D1053686

FINANCIAL SAVVY

for the

Small Business Owner

Financial Forum Publishing

Copies of this book are available for purchase through Financial Forum Bookstore. Discounts are given for volume purchases. For more information, call 435.750.0062, or go to www.ffbookstore.com

Publisher
Financial Forum Publishing and Communications
Tel: 435.750.0062
Email: info@ffpublish.com

DEDICATION

I dedicate this book to my mother and father — Ila and Kenneth J. Fisher — who taught me that everything is possible and the only limitations I have are the ones I put on myself. With their example of hard work, vision and an appreciation for life, itself, they have instilled in me the entrepreneurial spirit.

Lyn Fisher

To my mother, Catherine LeBlanc, who discovered little scraps of unintelligible poems in my room when I was 12, but encouraged me to continue writing and to pursue my career through almost insurmountable challenges. She taught me persistence through adversity and celebration through success, and continues to be a role model in my life. And to my late father, Robert LeBlanc (1923-1961) who showed me that ethics matters, especially when no one is looking.

Sydney LeBlanc

ACKNOWLEDGEMENT

Thanks to the staff at Financial Forum Publishing who spent countless hours to ensure a smooth completion of this project. A special thanks to project managers Cami Miller and Alison Hobbs.

.

TABLE OF CONTENTS

> *"The entrepreneur in us sees opportunities everywhere we look, but many people see only problems everywhere they look. The entrepreneur in us is more concerned with discriminating between opportunities than he or she is with failing to see the opportunities"*
>
> — Michael Gerber, author, entrepreneur

I'm a small business owner and proud of it. It's satisfying to know I had a dream, took hold of it and have worked hard to make it a reality. I have to admit it hasn't been easy. In fact, sometimes I wonder why I keep going. I work long hours, feel lots of stress and always have to be ready to put out "fires" as they occur. However, as I look at how far my business has come and the growth we have experienced, I feel a real sense of accomplishment

Not only can owning a business bring a sense of fulfillment to its owners/founders, but small businesses — with 500 or fewer employees, drive the U.S. economy by providing jobs for over half of the nation's private workforce. According to Thomas M. Sullivan, Chief Counsel for Advocacy, "Small business is a major part of our economy. Small businesses innovate and create new jobs at a faster rate than their larger competitors. They are nimble, creative, and a vital part of every community across the country."

A recent report presented by the SBA Office of Advocacy[1] shows those small firms:

- Represent 99.7% of all employer firms

- Employ about half of all private sector employees

- Pay nearly 45% of total U.S. private payroll

- Have generated 60-80% of net new jobs annually over the last decade

- Create more than half of nonfarm private gross domestic product (GDP)

- Hire 40% of high tech workers (such as scientists, engineers, and computer workers)

---

1 U.S. Dept. of Commerce, Bureau of the Census and International Trade Administration; Advocacy-funded research by Kathryn Kobe, 2007 (**www.sba.gov/advo/research/rs299tot.pdf**) and CHI Research, 2003 (**www.sba.gov/advo/research/rs225tot.pdf**); Federal Procurement Data System; U.S. Dept. of Labor, Bureau of Labor

- Are 52% home based and 2% franchises

- Made up 97.3% of all identified exporters and produced 28.9% of the known export value in 2006

- Produce 13 times more patents per employee than large patenting firms; these patents are twice as likely as large firm patents to be among the 1.0% most cited

So, what exactly is the description of a small business? It can be the revenue-generating website operated by a single mom who works from her home so she can spend more time with her children, the mom and pop store down on the corner, or it can be a 500-employee strong enterprise and anything in-between.

I'm an entrepreneur, as are most business owners. I recently completed an on-line questionnaire that rated my "entrepreneurial spirit." Do I have what it takes to be a successful business owner? Many of the questions were based on my ability to be a self-starter, the type of person who will take the bull by the horns and get the job done. I got 100% on the test and that qualified me as a "born entrepreneur whom, if I am not presently running my own business, should definitely start one — the sooner the better." It also said I was on my way to fame and riches. Oh, if it were only that easy.

While research shows that the number of non-employer firms (those with no employees) has risen steadily this decade, from 16.5 million in 2000 to an estimated 21.1 million in 2007 and employer firms have grown to an estimated 637,100, many of those new employer firms (560,300) closed that same year and 28,322 filed for bankruptcies.[2]

According to the same study, two-thirds of new employer establishments survive at least two years, 44% survive at least four years, and 31% survive at least seven years. Firms that began in the second quarter of 1998 were tracked for the next 28 quarters to determine their survival rate. Of special interest, the research found that businesses that survive four years have a better chance of surviving long-term. After the fourth year, the rate of firm closings declines considerably. Earlier research found that the major factors in a firm's survivability include an ample supply of capital, being large enough to have employees, the owner's education level, and the owner's reason for starting the firm.

---

2 Business Employment Dynamics Data: Survival and Longevity, II, by Amy E. Knaup and Merissa C. Piazza, *Monthly Labor Review*, vol. 30, no. 9 (Sept. 2007), pp. 3-10; Redefining Business Success: Distinguishing Between Closure and Failure by Brian Headd, *Small Business Economics*.

I find I am even more committed to my business because I have employees who depend on me to run my business properly. If the business fails, the lives of other people are affected. While this creates a lot of pressure for me, as the owner, it also gives me great pride to know that I am providing jobs for these skilled and talented people.

Since the mid-1990s, small businesses have created 60 to 80% of the net new jobs. In 2005, research showed that employer firms with fewer than 500 employees created 979,102 net new jobs, or 78.9%. Meanwhile, large firms with 500 or more employees added 262,326 net new jobs or 21.1%.[3]

Small businesses employ about half of U.S. workers. Of 116.3 million non-farm private sector workers in 2005, small firms with fewer than 500 workers employed 58.6 million and large firms employed 57.7 million. Firms with fewer than 20 employees employed 21.3 million. While small firms create 60 to 80% of net new jobs, their share of employment remains steady since some firms grow into large firms as they create new jobs.

As a small business owner, I realize that I can't do it alone. I depend on other professionals to guide me in areas where I lack the knowledge; e.g. financial advisor, CPA, attorney, mentors and coaches.

In compiling *Financial Savvy for the Small Business Owner* we invited a variety of professionals who work in and/or work with small businesses to share their knowledge on the topic of their expertise. These professionals understand the various needs of business owners, whether it is employee benefits and their usefulness as an employee retention and hiring tool, insurance and retirement needs, or even the things you need to know before exiting your business (business succession planning). And, of course, the book would not be complete without the more holistic aspects of business ownership that allow us to have a dream, keep our dream alive and rejoice as the dream becomes reality.

We hope you enjoy reading this book and find value in the pages within. And, most importantly, may your dreams become reality and your vision be your passion.

Lyn Fisher & Sydney LeBlanc

---

3 www.sba.gov/ advo/research/data.html#us.

1. ◆ Mistakes and Traps of Small Business Owners

Charles Auerbach, CFP®, CLU, ChFC, EA
David Williams, CFP®
Wealth Strategies Group, Inc.

There is a common misconception that as many as nine out of 10 new businesses close their doors in their first year of operation. Brian Headd, a researcher for the Small Business Administration, used U.S. Census Bureau data to come to the conclusion[1] that about half of new employer firms survive past four years. Of the businesses that closed, a third closed while successful. If business continuation also equals success, two out of three businesses are successful at the four-year mark.

So, do entrepreneurs have clear sailing? Not quite. Small business owners seem to fall into common mistakes or traps broadly categorized as problems of: Vision; Scale; Business Formalities; Cash Flow; Sales; Employees; Relationships; and Succession/ Exit Planning. This chapter will briefly discuss these categories and offer some ways to prevent or mitigate the problem.

Mistake #1: Vision

Vision implies looking ahead, having foresight, and watching where you are going. With businesses, we

---

1 Redefining Business Success: Distinguishing Between Closure and Failure." *Small Business Economics* 21, 2003,51-61.

need to know our status quo, where we want to end up, when we want to arrive, and how we plan to get there. That defines a business plan.

A properly written business plan is a living document. The business owner revises it every few years. It defines success, records the process to get there, and sets a time when that success goal should be met. As the business matures, the process may change, or the business owner may redefine success. He or she can set an exit date and plan on the value of his or her hard work being harvested or passed on.

The thought of writing down such a document intimidates many business owners. Instead, they choose to follow the unwritten business plan of: "Work hard. Make as much money as you can. Do it again next year. Hope for the best." But, if you don't document how you did it this year, how are you going to do it again next year? This unwritten plan also assumes you are going to work hard for as long as you live, and hope that your family, cherished ones and the business will be able to take care of themselves when you are gone. And, how will you know you have achieved success if you haven't determined what success is?

The business must create value for you
as well as for the customer.

Focus on why you started the business. What value do you want from it? If you started the business just to make money, then you can do that a whole lot easier working for someone else. But if you started the business to get control of your life, to express creativity, to make a difference, etc., then you can include this in your business plan as other markers for success.

Here is another issue with vision. Be careful that you don't blind yourself with your own brilliance. You and your team may, without a doubt, see the need for your new product or service, but if the buying public doesn't want it you're not going to sell it.

In the movie "Gremlins" Rand Peltzer is an inventor. He invents "The Bathroom Buddy." It has a shaving mirror, toothbrush, toothpick, toenail clippers, nail file, dental mirror, and a reservoir for toothpaste. He claims it eliminates the need to carry heavy luggage when you travel—and it is the invention of the century. The trouble is nobody wanted it.

Make sure you do market research before you invest assets in a project. Why should a customer buy your product or service? What's in it for them? If you can't determine and express the "value proposition," your customer won't be able to either. But, if you can articulate the return on investment for your product or service, the customer can justify the purchase. If you get enough positive feedback, go ahead — better yet, pre-sell the product or service to help fund the project.

Many entrepreneurs cloud their vision by having too many irons in the fire. They want to grab every piece of business they can get. When they fall prey to this lack of focus, they become a "jack of all trades, master of none." Their output becomes mediocre; they cease to provide value for their clients—and probably miss providing value for themselves. You need to keep focused on your core "competencies," the things you are good at and are part of your business plan.

Focusing on core competencies does not mean never expanding or diversifying. Just as a child grows and changes, so will your business grow and change. Just make sure you have planned for that change. Develop the strategies necessary to acquire core competencies for the expansion or diversification. Give as much thought to the growth plan as you did to the original written business plan.

> Keep focused on your core "competencies," the things you are good at and are part of your business plan.

While you are using your reflective brain to work out the details of business deals, don't ignore your reflexive brain. Our reflective brain processes all of the data we give it, but we cannot give it all of the data in real time to predict how humans will react within the deal. Our reflexive brain can react imperceptibly fast to make perceived risk decisions and character value judgments. It gives us our intuition, or "gut feeling." It's what keeps us alive while our reflective brain is entertaining us with plans and ideas. It stops us from going down that dark alley because something doesn't feel right; or keeps us away from that nice man who we learn later is a child molester. If your reflexive brain, "gut feeling," or intuition, tells you to stay away from a deal, listen to it.

Mistake #2: Scale

By scale, we are talking about the mental limitations you put on yourself and your business. That's not to say that the sky is the limit in everything. You need a framework (business plan) in which to work that defines upper goals and recognizes that you can "outdrive your headlights." However, owners often set unnecessary limitations on themselves out of fear of the unknown.

Avoid the mental limitation: "I'm not big enough to need a formal ownership structure." Sole proprietorship requires less paperwork and may provide a little tax savings in some states. However, as a sole proprietor, there is no separation between you and your business. Your personal assets and those of your family have no protection against legal demands made against the company. It is one thing for a claimant to get your business and all its assets; but as a sole proprietor, most everything you own or earn is up for grabs, too. (It can work the other way, too. A person who slips on the ice in front of your house can get the business.)

> **Create your business plan with reasonable growth expectations, and then go after the business.**

Of course, talk to your business attorney and business accountant when you choose a business entity. By structuring your business as an entity (e.g., Corporation or LLC), you create a separation between your businesses' liabilities and your personal assets. Working with a business entity may provide you with a degree of asset protection, it may make it easier to secure business credit, and it may give you more credibility in the marketplace.

You can put limitations on yourself and the business by thinking, acting, and speaking "small." Create your business plan with reasonable growth expectations, and then go after the business. If you can provide the goods and services, fulfill your promises, and are dependable, the customer will not care if you are a multi-national conglomerate or working out of your basement. You are not "small;" you are a boutique, you are personalized, you are nimble. You are a go-fast boat next to a container ship—you can maneuver faster, and provide your service in style.

Go-fast boats (also called "cigarette boats") can travel at speeds over 80 knots. They are stealthy, fast, and very difficult to intercept using conventional craft.

Don't get into the rut of "I've always done it this way." Automate and optimize. Take your processes apart every couple of years to see if you can do it faster, cheaper, or less often. Examine outsourcing. Your growth and profitability depends on optimizing.

Mistake #3: Business Formalities

Business owners often develop the attitude, "If it doesn't make me money, I don't want to be bothered with it." Unfortunately, when it comes to business formalities, "The devil is in the details." In other words, business formalities may not make you money, but it can really cost you if you don't follow through.

Earlier we mentioned the benefits of corporate or LLC structure. Unless you go through the motions of the business structure, authorities can say the structure doesn't exist. For example, a small corporation is often owned by a principal and spouse. They know the ownership split and they know who holds what ownership percentage, so they don't bother issuing stock certificates and creating a stock register. Without this proof of ownership, a court can claim that the company was acting like a sole proprietorship and should be treated as such in attaching assets in a lawsuit.

> Unless you go through the motions of the business structure, authorities can say the structure doesn't exist.

The same can be claimed if meetings of the directors and shareholders are not held and recorded. The initial meeting is the most important, because that is when all parties accept the Articles of Incorporation and Bylaws. It is like the birth of the new entity. Thereafter, a meeting should be held annually unless the Bylaws state that meetings are to be held at a different interval.

Since the corporation or LLC is a "person" in its own right, no one can speak for it unless the entity gives someone permission to do so. If a business wants to take out a business loan, the directors must meet to approve a written resolution authorizing an individual to borrow money for the corporation. You end up with a record of the minutes of that meeting and a signed written resolution. Without the written resolution, a lender can't lend to the corporation because no one has authority to bind the corporation to an agreement.

Do these formalities seem like a lot? Remember, you do these things to save your assets.

Many business owners wait until the tax return is prepared to control their income taxes. Very little can be done at that time, and none of the optimal strategies are available then. For example, retirement plan changes give an owner an excellent tool to control taxes, but those changes must be planned out before the beginning of the year. An owner and the company's accountant can determine which expenses should be claimed this year versus rolling them into next year, but this must be done before the expense is paid and before the end of the year. The tax ramifications of any change in income, expense, or capital transaction should be factored in as part of the determinants in implementation—although an owner shouldn't let the tax tail wag the business dog.

Mistake #4: Cash Flow Problems

Business consultants often say that "start-up business" and "undercapitalized business" are synonymous. Too often, small business owners simply underestimate the start-up costs and the time it takes to generate cash flow. They naturally use optimistic sales projections (both in amount and in timing), underestimate the expenses (including their own income need), and fail to take into consideration weak competitors who are willing to undercut their prices. Because of these pitfalls, one management consultant suggests that an aspiring entrepreneur calculate cash flow needs until the business is self-sustaining, and then multiply that number by three.

The quick and easy way to start a business is to use the owner's money. But, unless you are Lamar Hunt, that could be a problem.[2] As soon as possible, you need to separate your personal money from the business's money. Equity investors are one source of capital, but at the cost of giving up part ownership.

An owner needs to build a business credit profile early in the life of the company. Personally guaranteeing debts of the company or paying with a personal credit card does not build a business credit profile and potentially damages your personal credit rating as your debt-to-personal-income ratio increases. It takes time, persistence, and monitoring to create a business credit profile, but the results are worth it. Start by opening an account at a business supply store under your business name using your company's tax ID number, and use that account when you purchase necessary equipment and materials. Even if you can pay the account off in one payment, make

---

2 Lamar Hunt started the American Football League and the Dallas Texans in 1960. An apocryphal story says that the team lost a million dollars in the first year. A reporter went to Hunt's father and asked how he felt about his son losing a million dollars on a football team. Hunt's father smiled and said, "Certainly I'm worried. At that rate, Lamar will be broke in 250 years."

timely payments over a 90- to 120-day period. You will also want to make sure that the vendor reports your credit under the business name.

Only after you can prove that your business has a history of on-time payment with vendors do you want to register with the major business credit reporting agencies. Dun and Bradstreet is the biggest company, but Experian Business, Business Credit USA, Client Checker, Equifax Business and FD Insight also serve this market.

When it comes to operating cash flow, many business owners become Jack Benny. However, you must be careful of false economy. Some expenses generate a return on investment (ROI), and the saying is mostly true: "You get what you pay for." It's hard to be objective during the start-up period of the business, so get a second opinion on discretionary or capital-related expenditures.

We often think: "Why pay someone to do something I can do myself?" This is dangerous thinking for a business owner. Business tasks that are not key to income generation may be done more efficiently if you outsource them. Can you earn more attending to your business during the time freed up than you are by paying someone to handle the task? That is positive ROI and so handing the task off is worthwhile.

> It's hard to be objective during the start-up period of the business, so get a second opinion on discretionary or capital-related expenditures.

Tools trade time for money. Buying better commercial-grade tools and technology will pay for themselves in faster and better output, lower labor costs, and happier customers. This is another example of positive ROI.

Offering above-average compensation will get you above-average employees who are faster, happier, and better with your customers. For certain classes of employees, making a part of the compensation performance-based can improve cash flow, as you pay the above-average compensation after you have received the benefit of the above-average productivity. Above-average management eliminates below-average employees.

Mistake #5: Sales

Businesses fail because they didn't have enough in sales, and they fail if they had too many sales. It all depends on where the business is in its development cycle. A start-up business needs to focus almost exclusively on sales. If sales grow, expenses will take care of themselves. However, once cash flow is being generated from sales, the business owner needs to shift attention to infrastructure and fulfillment.

Chrysler gave us an object lesson on sales growth that was too fast. The 1957 "Forward Design" models were very popular with their push-button transmissions, torsion bar suspension, and large fins (Chrysler called them "stabilizers"). These technologically advanced cars were so popular that the company could not keep up with demand. The assembly lines and their workers were sped up — the result was cars that fell apart before they made it to the dealer's lot.

Some start-up business owners are so eager for the sale they will try to sell their product to anyone who can fog a mirror. There are clients you don't want: slow payers; overly cost-sensitive; more trouble that they are worth; or, just hard to work with. Avoid these customers; better yet, refer your competitors to them.

You don't have to spend time with everyone who is interested in you. You don't have to network just because you are "supposed to" network.

If you can't see a way of doing business with someone, don't meet with him or her to "see if there's a way we can do something together."

Be careful that you don't become economically dependent on a small group of related customers. If more than 50% of your sales come from one customer, you become vulnerable. Often, that one client makes inordinate demands on your time and resources so that your other clients suffer and you don't have time to develop additional customers. Remember, such customers are less dependent on you than you are on them. The business could leave for any one of a multitude of reasons.

More than one company has failed from what could be labeled the "Wal-Mart syndrome." Many business owners think that they can jumpstart their business if they become the low-cost leader. You need to prove your value as a new and small brand. If you are cheap, you may get some business from the bottom feeders, but many more customers will avoid you because they know they get what they pay for. Your fixed expenses (including your income need) do not drop when you lower the price, so lower price yields lower profit. You can't lose 25-cents on each item, but make it up in volume.

Know which part of your market will generate the greatest profit. It is not always the top of the line product or service. This is where market testing and your business plan come in. Selling 10 items with a markup of $100 each is better than selling 50 items with a $10 markup or one item with a $500 markup.

Mistake #6: Employees

In a small business employees are its biggest asset. It's important to hire the right ones, but even more important to keep them. A good employee becomes more valuable over time, as he or she increases in skills and industry knowledge and increases in company-specific knowledge. As the workforce ages and leaves the workplace, companies have lost vast storehouses of knowledge. They realize too late that they didn't have a mechanism in place to pass that information on to the next generation of workers. Learn from the mistakes of large companies; document operational procedures and cross-train employees.

Make sure you have a system in place to reward your employees for their efforts.

In an old British sitcom, the elderly storeowner had very specific staff selection criteria for his secretaries. He would have his candidates show a bit of leg. If his heart monitor didn't go off she didn't get the job. This was irrelevant staff selection criteria (and a lawsuit waiting to happen). A small business owner can easily get caught in the irrelevant staff selection trap when anything other than job description and skill proficiency is used in selecting new hires.

This is especially true in family owned and run businesses. An adult child who has worked for years in the business is not automatically CEO material. While family dynamics are a powerful force, the business owner has to decide which is more important: a happy nephew or a business that survives after the owner's exit.

Just as irrelevant staff selection needs to be avoided while hiring, irrelevant staff selection can destroy a company when staff reduction is necessary. Two common irrelevant criteria are family and the highest paid employees. Family may be retained to keep peace at the cost of those who really do the work. Firing the highest paid employees may give you the greatest reduction in payroll, but you must remember that these employees earn the highest compensation because they give you the greatest return.

If you want to reduce staff in the worst way, let a rumor start that there will be layoffs. Your most competent employees will polish their résumés and find jobs first. You will be left with a smaller staff — all those who couldn't get hired anywhere else.

The owner of a small business usually starts out doing everything. As employees are hired, the owner needs to shift from production to management. You need to learn the care and feeding of good employees. Like a good employee, you also need to improve skills. Over time, you need to become an executive, able to groom management to care for the business when you can't be there. Ultimately, you need to put in place an executive and management team to provide continuity of business when you finally leave the company.

Mistake #7: Relationships

As a small business owner, whatever industry or market you are in, it's a "people business." You have to manage relationships both inside and outside the business.

Importance of Employee Supervision

The owner of one of my favorite restaurants went to Europe for a few months to learn new recipes and cooking styles. He came back in time to see the sheriff nail liens on the restaurant door, which never reopened. His employees skimmed the till rather than pay bills. Another person, the owner of a commercial products company, had to take an extended absence to care for a major health problem. He returned to a business that had lost a third of its revenue. The employees weren't dishonest—they just weren't motivated.

Both stories are over-simplified, but they indicate the importance of supervision by someone who has ownership in the business. That ownership can be emotional or financial and still be effective, although a dollar beats a warm fuzzy feeling in my book. ◆

It is difficult to fire under-performing employees. It becomes doubly hard when they are family. Some get consumed by their emotions and make business decisions for the wrong reasons — and doing nothing is a decision. You must rely on facts and sound business judgment to make good decisions.

When a small business owner has to partner with someone who is providing equal value, it seems that the fair thing to do is to create a 50/50 partnership. This is a recipe for disaster. No one has control of the business. If the partners should disagree on a matter of substance, no one can make a final decision and the business goes nowhere. A 51/49 split gives someone veto power, and the 51% partner should act as CEO. If the partners must be equal, give 2% to a disinterested advisor in a 49/49/2 partnership. The two partners operate the business — the 2% advisor would get called in as a tie-breaker.

Business is built and run on relationships.

Some say that the word, "company" derives from the Latin com (with) plus panis (bread) — indicating that the Romans knew the importance of the business lunch. In any business transaction that takes time to complete, it is the relationship of the parties that gets things done. The formality of a contract or agreement helps protect a relationship or gives a basis from which to resolve disputes, but the end result almost always strays from that contract as each party interacts with the other. No matter how ironclad a contract may be, the relationship will rule. You must feel comfortable with the other party in proportion to the criticalness of the transaction. Contracts and agreements are broken all of the time between parties where the relationship was lost — the trust was lost, or one party never intended to enter into a true relationship.

People want to do business with a person, not a business. So a business owner must cultivate relationships with customers, and they must train their employees to nurture these relationships as well. Customers are expecting more and more "high touch" service from those they do business with. Small business can provide that personal attention easier than a large corporation, and this is where you can shine.

Mistake #8: Planning for Succession and Exit

Up to this point we have emphasized the issues involved in starting, operating, and growing a small business. By avoiding or surviving the mistakes and traps mentioned, you end up with a profitable business.

The last trap is embodied in the fact that every business owner will leave the business, whether they want to or not. If you want your business to continue in order to benefit your family and others, you must find answers to the following questions:

- Who will own and operate your business if you die prematurely?
- Who will run your business if you become incapacitated?
- How do you get out of the business alive — harvesting its value for return on your blood, sweat and tears?

- Who will be the successor owners and operators?

Just as there is an unwritten default business plan, there is an unwritten default succession and exit plan—do nothing. The default plan allows you to lock in the lowest value for your business and the highest tax payment to the government. Continuation, succession, and exit planning have two components: non-tax considerations and tax ramifications. Addressing the intricacies of the first and mitigating the effects of the latter are best handled over a period of time.

The non-tax considerations in succession and exit planning become especially critical when family members are involved. Studies[3] indicate that only 30% of family businesses survive into the second generation, only 12% survive into the third generation, and only 3% survive into the fourth generation and beyond. Yet, it is possible for the business to end successfully at any of these generations with advance planning.

There are six areas of tension in family businesses which become pronounced at a succession or exit event:

1. Resistance of the older generation to retire or to relinquish control after retirement

2. Participating and non-participating heirs expect to benefit from the business

3. Sibling rivalry

4. Emotion (nostalgia) and control issues

5. Introduction of outsiders into the family's business

6. Fear of estate and gift taxes

All of these can be moderated if planning is done in advance.

A succession plan requires a commitment from all parties involved. Family members may be willing to work together if they recognize the ramifications of the unwritten default succession plan. All parties have to set aside their competitiveness so that they can work together rather than tear the business apart.

A company needs a mission statement and a strategic plan. The strategic plan spells out at what point the business would be sold or transferred so that all parties know when a change may come, and the mission statement

---

3 Beckhard, R. and Dyer, W. G., Jr. Managing Continuity in the Family-Owned Business. *Organizational Dynamics*, 12 (1), 1983, 5-12; Kenyon-Rouvinez. Patterns in Serial Business Families: Theory Building Through Global Case Study Research. *Family Business Review*, 14 (3), 2001, 175-192.

sets out what values will be used to get to the goal. The family needs a financial plan and a mission statement so that all in the family know what goals they are working toward within the family.

Personal development plans must be developed for family members expected to hold management and executive positions. If key employees are expected to fit into the succession or exit plan, a culture needs to be created within the company that creates the feeling of ownership in them.

Agreements, entities, and other legal structures need to be put in place well before a transfer might occur. Financial arrangements must be made in advance so that the legal structures can be properly funded. The earlier that succession and exit planning can begin, the better.

A sale or transfer of a business will trigger income tax, capital gains tax, and gift or estate tax to one degree or another. The tax consequences can be controlled in each of the three areas with advance planning. Often, controlling when the taxes are realized through tax deferral or gifting can substantially reduce taxes owed. Tax law permits you to discount the value of parts of your business for tax purposes without affecting the actual value of the company. Consulting early with your tax advisor and business attorney will allow you to legally get ownership to the people you intend to at the lowest tax cost, leaving more for yourself and your heirs.

Not Admitting Your Mistakes

We have quickly touched on a number of traps and mistakes that businesses make. Chrysler, IBM, Quaker Oats, and many more businesses have made these mistakes and survived. Studebaker, Drexel Burnham Lambert, Eastern Airlines, and many more businesses made these mistakes and are no longer with us. These traps and mistakes are part of the business environment. You will make some of them yourself.

The key is to act as soon as you realize that things are going wrong. The longer any of these issues are permitted to go on, the more expensive it will be to fix. Don't let pride get in your way—write out a plan that will set out the steps necessary to fix, change directions, or accept the limitations you now face. Forewarned is forearmed. By taking corrective action early on you, too, may be part of the two out of three businesses that are considered successful.

Charles Auerbach, CFP®, CLU, ChFC, EA
President and Co-Founder
Wealth Strategies Group, Inc.
8001 Centerview Parkway, Ste. 201
Cordova, TN 38018
Tel: 901.473.9000 Ext. 104
Fax: 901.473.9008
Email: Charlie.auerbach@natplan.com
www.wealthstrategiesgrouptn.com

ABOUT THE AUTHOR: Charles Auerbach is President and co-founder of Wealth Strategies Group, Inc. in Cordova, Tennessee, and an Investment Advisor Associate with Wealth Strategies Advisory Group, Inc. Charlie has more than 30 years experience in the financial field.

After receiving a Bachelor of Science in Accounting at Brooklyn College in New York in 1971, he worked for the Internal Revenue Service in New York, New York until 1983. His IRS positions included Revenue Agent, Audit Reviewer, and Appellate Conference.

In 1983, Charlie became the Due Diligence Officer at Morgan Keegan in Memphis, where he remained until 1994 when he co-founded Jaffe Auerbach Advisory Group and served as its Chief Operations Officer until 2001. With a shared vision of personalized, comprehensive financial service to a selective clientele, Charlie and his Partner, Steve Silver, co-founded Wealth Strategies Group, Inc. and Wealth Strategies Advisory Group, Inc.

Charlie has special interest in business planning, strategic philanthropy, and values-based legacy planning. He presently serves as Development Chairman and Past President of the Board of United Cerebral Palsy, Mid-South Chapter. He currently serves on the Professional Advisory Group of the Memphis Jewish Foundation and is a member of the Association of Fund Raising Professionals. Charlie has also served as Past President of the Mid-South Chapter of the Financial Planning Association and of the Temple Israel Brotherhood.

David Williams, CFP®
Registered Investment Associate
Wealth Strategies Group, Inc.
Email: Dave@WSG-TN.com

ABOUT THE AUTHOR: David Williams is an RIA with Wealth Strategies Advisory Group, Inc. Prior to establishing his business consultancy, he was Director of Financial Planning for Regions Morgan Keegan Trust.

Dave has devoted the last four years to consulting with businesses and their executives through his firm, Business Enhancement Associates, LLC. He helps business owners and corporations grow, protect, and transfer wealth. Dave has more than 25 years experience as a financial planner dealing primarily with business owners. He has developed special expertise in advanced estate and charitable planning, employer stock option planning, and qualified plans.

Which Business Entity is Best for You?

Charles Young, CPA

Business Entity: the structure and accounting records reflect the financial activities of a specific corporate entity, separate and distinct from the people who finance it or work in it.

As a small business owner, you have several choices when selecting the entity your business will run under. The most common are: Sole Proprietorship, Partnership, C Corporation, S Corporation, Limited Liability Partnership and Limited Liability Company. Following is a review of some of the characteristics of each entity and what to consider when making your choice.

C Corporation: Small businesses typically decide against a C Corporation because there are two levels of tax imposed on C Corporation income. The C Corporation pays income tax on its taxable income when it files its federal corporate tax return. Then when the C Corporation distributes its earnings to the shareholders as dividends, the shareholder reports those dividends on his/her tax return as taxable income. Together, these two levels of taxes are referred to as "double taxation". State income taxes may also apply. Generally, a C Corporation is not the preferred entity for small businesses.

Sole Proprietor: Operating as a sole proprietor is the easiest form of doing business. It eliminates the C Corporation double taxation issue. You only pay individual taxes on your net profits. However, as a sole proprietor, you lack the legal protection that corporate status gives you. Owners of corporations have limited liability, but sole proprietors do not. Therefore, if you're a sole-proprietor, your personal assets are at risk if the business is sued.

LLP: Similar in may aspects to the LLC. However, one key difference is that LLPs must have at least two owners and are taxed under the complicated partnership tax rules. So one individual can't own a partnership.

For small businesses then the choice narrows to either an LLC or an S Corporation.

LLC and S Corporation: Both are "pass-through" entities. This means that generally, neither entity pays corporate taxes. Net profits are reported by the owners on their individual tax returns. Also both offer limited liability protection. Your liability will be limited to your investment in either entity.

When choosing between an S Corporation and an LLC there are some additional items to consider.

- S Corporation status is a way to avoid the C Corporation double taxation issue. As a pass-through entity the S Corporation income is taxed personally to the shareholders. You also get limited liability protection meaning you are limited to losing your investment in the S Corporation and not your personal investments.

- The S Corporation is still a corporation. S Corporation shareholders have all of the same legal protections as C Corporation shareholders. The S Corporation is a federal tax law concept. To be taxed under the federal S Corporation tax rules the corporation makes an election by filing federal tax Form 2553. Once you have elected S Corporation status, it is difficult to change to an LLC if you decide later to make the switch. You would first have to liquidate the S Corporation potentially generating taxable gains for the shareholders.

- By default, Limited Liability Companies (LLCs) with at least two owners (members) are taxed as partnerships. LLCs with only one owner (member), the single-member LLC, are taxed as sole proprietorships. As with S Corporations, the LLC is a pass-through entity and the owner reports the LLC income on his/her personal tax return. However, it is much easier to switch to an S Corporation later. The LLC simply files Form 2553 to elect S Corporation status without having to liquidate.

Differences between S Corporations and LLCs

An S Corporation can have no more than 100 shareholders, and only certain types of shareholders can own an S Corporation, incuding: individuals, estates, and qualifying trusts. Non-resident aliens cannot be S Corporation shareholders.

S Corporations can have only one class of stock. The income and expenses from an S Corporation, as well as any distributions paid to shareholders, are allocated based on the shareholder's ownership percentage. The S Corporation net income reported on the shareholder's personal tax return is not subject to self-employment taxes. And S Corporation shareholders who are active in the business must be paid a reasonable salary.

The amount of your investment in the S Corporation, referred to as your cost basis, is calculated as follows:

- Increased by your contributions of cash and property

- Increased (decreased) by your share of S Corporation profits (losses)

- Decreased by your share of distributions

- Increased by loans made directly to the corporation by you

This cost basis calculation is your tax cost. The higher your basis the more losses you can claim on your personal tax return.

LLCs, taxed as partnerships, are more flexible than S Corporations. There is no limit on the number of owners and any person, business, or trust can be an owner. With an LLC you can make special allocations with particular types of income and expenses among owners. The status of the business's net income reported on the owner's personal tax return that is subject to self-employment tax is unsettled tax law. Current thinking is that some of the taxable income, representing reasonable compensation paid in the form of guaranteed payments to owners active in the business, is subject to self-employment tax.

Your cost basis in an LLC is calculated as follows:

- Increased by your contributions of cash and property

- Increased (decreased) by your share of LLC profits (losses)

- Decreased by your share of distributions

- Increased by your share of the LLCs debts (if you are personally liable for the debts).

The advantage of LLCs over S Corporations is the ability to increase the owner's cost basis in the LLC for LLC debts the LLC owner is personally liable for.

Conclusion

Often, it's a good idea for a business to start as an LLC. LLC's are flexible, LLC owners may be able to take more LLC losses on their personal tax returns, and LLC's can easily switch to an S Corporation later.

However, it is always wise to consult an attorney, tax expert or other financial professional before making a final decision as to which business entity you will use. They will evaluate your personal situation and help you with the process.

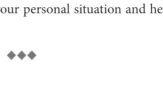

2. How Small Business Owners Can Use Benefits to Achieve Business Objectives

Dr. Ronald S. Leopold and Robert D. Bucci
MetLife

Workplace benefits can be used as an important business driver now, and their role will continue to grow in importance to both employers and employees as macro and micro economic and demographic trends continue to reshape workplace expectations and needs on the part of both groups.

Workplace benefits are viewed as an important employee retention tool by small businesses. More than half (55%) of smaller employers, those with fewer than 500 employees, say benefits play a very important role in employee retention — a top objective, according to MetLife's sixth annual Study of Employee Benefits Trends (2008)[1]. However, many current benefits programs being offered by smaller employers may not be utilized to their full retention potential. According to the MetLife study, only about one-third (34%) of workers at these smaller employers say the benefits they receive are a very important reason to remain with their employer, contrasted to more than half (53%) of employees working at larger companies. In addition, just 37% of employees at smaller companies, compared to 49% of employees at larger firms, say they are highly satisfied with their workplace benefits.

1 MetLife's sixth annual Employee Benefits Trends Study referenced in this chapter can be obtained at whymetlife.com/trendspr along with a wealth of other related resources.

While small businesses are recognizing that investing in benefits is a strategic decision, many current benefits programs are not meeting the wants and needs of today's workforce and not contributing as they could to employee satisfaction and retention. Small employers may not have the economies of scale to offer some of the employer-paid benefits and programs of their larger counterparts in an economical fashion; however, there is much more that they can be doing — without a significant financial investment. For example, supporting voluntary benefits in the workplace can help address the challenge of expanding the breadth and depth of a benefits program to improve employee satisfaction without adding notably to the employer's overall benefits spend.

Because key megatrends, including the aging population and the escalating cost of health care coverage, are profoundly impacting the relationship between employers and employees, it is suggested that small business owners take time now to think through the following benefits issues and engage in dialogue with their management teams, consultants or brokers.

Here are eight suggested conversation starters:

1. How the employer's benefits role is changing

2. Benefits that can address retention and cost control challenges

3. Utilizing non-medical benefits to their full potential

4. How employee choice affects the equation

5. Educating employees on the value of risk protection

6. How to help employees understand their personal responsibility

7. Benefits programs that appeal to your unique workforce

8. Tying improved employee satisfaction to profitability

After reading the insights behind each of these eight conversation starters, employers should have a better understanding of how their benefits program can help position them to compete for the best talent, as well as potential ways to maximize every dollar spent on benefits – increasing the likelihood that their benefits investment will provide a meaningful return to their company's bottom line.

How the Employer's Benefits Role is Changing

Small business owners should be considering benefits as an investment in their business, rather than merely as an expense. An investment, as we all know, has the potential of bringing returns greater than the initial outlay. This mindset is important for using benefits strategically because the MetLife study actually revealed that smaller employers *proportionally* are paying more for benefits than larger competitors, yet their return on that investment is less. Without the advantage of economies of scale, smaller employers need to be innovative in their benefits implementation – from the inclusion of voluntary benefits, to adding health and wellness programs, to increasing the flexibility of schedules to permit greater work/life balance for employees. Hand-in-hand with this are improved benefits communications and decision support tools. These are essential for helping employees understand their options and gain a greater appreciation of their workplace benefits, which, in turn, can help small employers obtain a better return on their same benefits investment. (See Employee Loyalty on page 22.)

Employees are looking for help in securing their personal safety net. The workplace has become the dominant starting point for this effort. According to MetLife's Study of Employee Benefits Trends, more than half of working Americans (52%) are obtaining the majority of their financial and retirement products through the workplace. Employees want the ability to choose from a broader set of benefits, even if that means shouldering the financial burden. According to the 2008 MetLife Study of the American Dream, more than 90% of Americans believe that it is important for companies to continue to offer benefits, even if employees must pay most or all of the costs. Nearly three-quarters of those surveyed, 71%, said it was *very important.*

Employees' financial concerns have also prompted their interest for more advice and guidance — and they are looking to the workplace to be that source of information. They are interested in having their employers provide access to guidance on a range of issues — from general financial needs to planning retirement, and making informed decisions about company benefits. For example, according to MetLife's Study of Employee Benefits Trends almost half of employees want access to financial planners and benefits advisors at the workplace. Employers that can support their workers in taking action are more likely to keep their most talented workers, particularly as benefits satisfaction proves to be an even more important factor in addressing employee loyalty and retention goals than ever before.

Employee Loyalty

According to the MetLife Study of Employee Benefits Trends, a majority (60%) of smaller employers — those with less than 500 employees — say they have a strong sense of loyalty to their employees compared to 45% of larger companies. Yet, this sense of loyalty is not being felt by many employees — only 44% of workers at these smaller companies believe that their employer has very strong sense of loyalty to them. This is despite another of the study's findings that, among employers that offer benefits, a higher percentage of smaller employers, contrasted to larger employers, are paying all of the costs for many benefits including medical, dental, vision and prescription drugs.

For example, more than one-third of smaller employers (36%) that offer benefits say they pay the entire share of employees' medical coverage and 29% pay all the cost of prescription drug coverage compared to only 15% and 13%, respectively, among employers with 500 plus employees. Breadth and depth of benefits offerings may have greater impact on employee loyalty than cost-sharing proportions. Employees at smaller companies indicate an interest in paying more to get more — 91% of those surveyed say they are interested in having more voluntary benefits offered with 40% saying they are very interested. ◆

Employers Paying All Costs for Medical & Drug Benefits

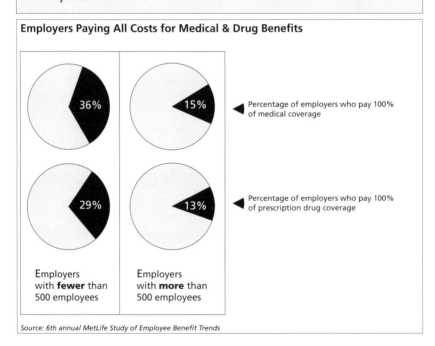

Percentage of employers who pay 100% of medical coverage

Percentage of employers who pay 100% of prescription drug coverage

Employers with **fewer** than 500 employees

Employers with **more** than 500 employees

Source: 6th annual MetLife Study of Employee Benefit Trends

What do all these trends mean for U.S. employers? Simply put: opportunities —

Opportunities to use benefits more strategically to help satisfy employees' needs as well as the company's own business needs.

Employees are looking to employers for more financial protection products and access to information and guidance, and employers that attempt to meet these new demands are likely to find the rewards surpass the efforts.

Benefits Help Address Retention and Cost Control Challenges

Across all employers surveyed for the MetLife Study of Employee Benefits Trends, retention and cost control were the top two benefits objectives. However, concerns of employee retention are felt more strongly among smaller employers than larger ones. For example, 59% of employers with fewer than 500 employees said employee retention was their most important benefits objective contrasted with 46% of employers with 500 or more employees.

Small businesses that are lean on headcount may find productivity is seriously impacted when one or more employees leave. The leaving, of course, can be for myriad reasons, but there are some reasons that an employer has more control over than others. What can you do to help retain your employees for the long term? What role can your benefits program play in helping to generate employee loyalty that can be critical to retaining talent? MetLife research has revealed a correlation between employee benefits satisfaction and loyalty to employers. The study found that among employees who are highly satisfied with their benefits, 70% say benefits are an important reason to remain with an employer, compared to just 14% among those who are not satisfied with their benefits.

Employees' benefits needs and desires are as diverse as the employers that they work for. Understanding the needs and wants of employees based on key demographic information such as age and life stage is helpful. For example, while dental insurance ranks as the fifth most important benefit among all employees, it is the second most important benefit among young singles (ages 21 through 34). Among these younger workers, dental benefits are valued slightly more than vacation time. So, for instance, if new college graduates are among those you are trying to recruit, you may want to take a closer look at this demographic's benefits preferences.

While many small businesses may find that medical costs consume so many dollars that the added costs for a dental plan are difficult to manage, *not* providing dental coverage can have both direct and indirect costs for the employer. Not only can employee loyalty and retention dynamics be potentially strengthened with an enhanced benefits program, but also poor oral health could potentially lead to a host of medical conditions. These medical conditions can potentially impact your employees' out-of-pocket finances as well as your company's medical, disability, and absenteeism-related costs.

While a MetLife Oral Health Study found that most consumers (85%) believe there is a strong connection between oral health and overall medical health, we also know that people without dental benefits are less likely to visit the dentist. According to MetLife's Employee Benefits Trends Study, half of people without dental benefits will not see a dentist. However, only a little more than half (58%) of employers with 2 to 49 employees offer dental coverage. That number rises to 69% for employers with fewer than 500 employees, and escalates to 90% for employers with 500 or more employees. Also, while working for small businesses can have great appeal for seasoned executives at larger companies who are transitioning to retirement — for example, they like the more flexible work schedules in retirement — loss of key benefits in a tight economic climate may be an obstacle to those considering the change.

MetLife research has found that medical coverage consistently is considered the most important benefit by employees across different age groups and family situations.

How can an employer reap the benefits of offering dental coverage (and other valued benefits) and do this with an eye to price sensitivity? One such way is with voluntary benefits. Voluntary benefits, where the employee pays most or all of the cost of the premium, is one way to help address the challenge of expanding the breadth and depth of a benefits program to improve employee satisfaction without adding notably to the employer's overall benefits spend. Continuing with the dental example, a voluntary dental plan can be designed to cover preventive and diagnostic services, with more cost sharing for the more expensive services, which are also more elective. In addition, providing employees with educational materials about the importance of good oral health may help encourage participants to maintain regular preventive care — mitigating larger expenses for all stakeholders.

Utilizing Non-Medical Benefits to Their Full Potential

It likely comes as no surprise that while employees' benefits preferences are influenced by their age, marital status, and other life stage factors, MetLife research has found that medical coverage consistently is considered the most important benefit by employees across different age groups and family situations. Employers of all sizes seem to understand the importance of providing medical insurance. MetLife research shows that approximately 95% of all employers provide medical coverage. However, since the vast majority of employers provide some form of medical coverage, one can see that it is not necessarily a point of differentiation for employees comparing one employer to the next. It is considered the "norm" or "table stakes."

In MetLife's study, employees were asked about the importance of benefits in retention and workplace loyalty. Employees indicated salary/wages were number one, health benefits were number two, and retirement benefits and advancement opportunities were tied for the third most critical factor. However, many employers are not realizing the importance of retirement benefits as a loyalty driver — whereas 72% of employees say retirement benefits are an important factor in loyalty, only 41% of employers say the same. By having insights into the drivers of employee loyalty, employers of all sizes can more strategically optimize their benefits offerings. Understanding the important role other benefits can play in broadening the breadth and depth of a benefits program can be a competitive advantage.

Another item to consider is how other benefits can offer financial protection against unexpected health events or situations, such as disability, dental, life, critical illness and long-term care insurance. These can fill in the gaps that medical insurance was not designed to cover and can help employees achieve a strong financial safety net. With the importance employees place on health insurance, these benefits should be a supplement to medical coverage, not a replacement. For example, critical illness survival is on the rise as demonstrated by scientific and medical breakthroughs, but there are new financial challenges. An employee confronted with a critical illness can also confront a spike in expenses not covered by traditional medical coverage. According to the MetLife study:

The top financial concern among full-time employees is having enough money to pay bills during a period of sudden income loss.

How Employee Choice Affects the Equation

With the diversity of employee populations and their respective employers, a one-size-fits-all benefits program can be ineffective and inefficient. Today's small employers can find that insurers have been able to harness the efficiencies of technology to now offer increased flexibility and value-added benefits options on many key protection products.

Voluntary benefits, cafeteria arrangements and other benefits platforms that allow greater flexibility and choice are likely to become increasingly attractive to both employers and their employees. They help employers optimize the inherent value of benefits plans by expanding the number of coverage options available to employees for selection (breadth of coverage) as well as allowing individuals to "buy-up" to higher levels of protection to fit their needs (depth of coverage). By giving employees access to some level of customization can help ensure that employers' benefits plans are more likely to satisfy a diverse constituency and have a positive business impact.

Educating Employees on the Value of Risk Protection

Regardless of their employer's size, some personal issues confront all employees. The MetLife study found that about one-third of all employees say they have a limited amount of time to do necessary research to help them make financial decisions — likely a reason why only about one-third express confidence in their ability to make the right financial decisions for their families. Money is also a concern regardless of employer size — about four in ten employees say they live paycheck to paycheck. So with time availability, money and confidence levels on par, it may come as a surprise that fewer employees at smaller companies have taken steps to determine their family's financial needs in relation to financial protection such as life insurance, retirement income and disability income insurance than their neighbors at larger employers. (See chart on page 27.)

American households are continuing to face growing financial exposure and risk — higher household health care bills, growing concerns about Social Security and Medicare financial solvency, as well as a growing reliance on two incomes rather than one to sustain many households' standard of living have become the new norm. Workplace benefits are likely to continue to grow in perceived value by a workforce that is becoming aware of greater future risks. Benefits can already be seen play-

Employees' Action Steps by Employer Size

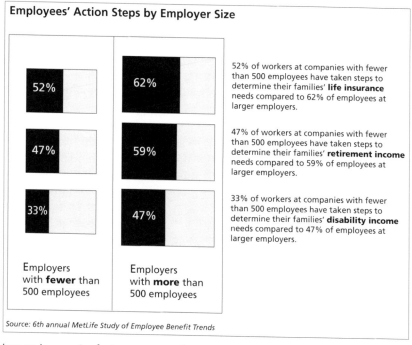

52% of workers at companies with fewer than 500 employees have taken steps to determine their families' **life insurance** needs compared to 62% of employees at larger employers.

47% of workers at companies with fewer than 500 employees have taken steps to determine their families' **retirement income** needs compared to 59% of employees at larger employers.

33% of workers at companies with fewer than 500 employees have taken steps to determine their families' **disability income** needs compared to 47% of employees at larger employers.

Employers with **fewer** than 500 employees

Employers with **more** than 500 employees

Source: 6th annual MetLife Study of Employee Benefit Trends

ing an increasingly important role in employees' decisions to remain with their employer. In 2007, 45% of surveyed employees said benefits were an important reason why they remain with their current employer, up from 33% a year before. An additional one-third (33%) said benefits were an important factor attracting them to their current job, up from 28% the previous year.

Communication of benefits and the value they provide is essential part of the equation as well, and both smaller employers and their employees are in agreement that benefits communications is an area that needs improvement. Only about one-third of employers (with fewer than 500 employees) and their employees believe that current benefits communications are highly effective. More than half (54%) of employees at these smaller businesses say receiving personalized benefits information with costs for options would make it easier when making choices.

Helping Employees Understand Their Personal Responsibility

The health of your employees not only impacts your company's bottom line but also their own finances. Since medical expenses continue to grow, employees' out-of-pocket component will likely increase as well. It is important that employees understand the need to anticipate and protect against unexpected medical events and situations, but there are actions that they can also take to mitigate the potential for more serious illnesses and chronic absences through healthy lifestyle choices such as appropriate diet and exercise, and participating in offered wellness and disease management programs.

Education is essential because health *insurance* is not health *assurance*. In other words, while health insurance can offer employees important financial protection for acute medical events, it was not designed to help employees and their employers take a preventive approach to serious conditions that can often be avoided with healthy lifestyle decisions.

> *Helping employees see the value of wellness programs can lead to employee engagement and improved participation that can benefit all stakeholders.*

Small employers have room for growth when it comes to wellness programs. The MetLife study found that more than half (57%) of larger employers (those with 500 or more employees) in 2007 were providing employees with a wellness program up from 49% in 2006. However, the number of smaller employers (those with fewer than 500 employees) who offer a wellness program has remained steady over the two-year period at about one in five (16%). Approximately nine out of 10 companies, both large and small, who offer a wellness program, believe they are effective for reducing medical costs. Consider how these programs can affect even the smallest employers as almost two-thirds of companies with two to 49 employees are spending 60% or more of their total benefits spend on medical insurance. Investing in wellness and disease management programs appropriate for your particular workforce and communicating frequently about them can help employees not only understand their personal responsibility, but also take an active role in the benefits equation.

Benefits Programs That Appeal to Your Unique Workforce

As mentioned previously, benefits preferences and needs can be influenced by age, life stage, family status, and gender among other factors. For example, baby boomers can find long-term care insurance a valuable protection to help ensure that retirement savings are kept intact. However, more than half (56%) of baby boomers do not own long-term care insurance, and 68% have not taken steps to determine their long-term care insurance needs. Companies looking to meet the needs of their baby boomer employees may want to consider making this coverage — and educational materials and communications supporting it — available.

Young families with children under the age of six, on the other hand, may find life insurance benefits particularly valuable — 61% of young families are very concerned about having financial security for their family in the event of premature death. Since 60% of young families are also concerned about paying for their children's education, communications geared toward young families can illustrate how life insurance protection can help ensure funding for children's future college expenses and their other financial needs in the case of a parent's death.

Gender can also be a key factor to consider when building a benefits program and communications plan. MetLife's Study of Employee Benefits Trends revealed that, in general, female employees who have life insurance own only two times their household income in coverage while male employees with life insurance generally have three times their household income in coverage. This gender gap is surprising given that 64% of working women vs. 52% of working men are very concerned about their families' financial futures in the event of their own premature death. Since only 69% of employers with fewer than 500 employees offer life insurance (compared to 92% of employers with 500-plus employees who offer it) voluntary benefits can again be used to advantage to add this coverage to an employer's benefits portfolio. Female employees may look to the workplace as a source of supplemental coverage purchase options. In fact, 52% of women cite the convenience of buying voluntary benefits through the workplace as an important advantage.

Tying Improved Employee Satisfaction to Profitability

Research points to a correlation between benefits satisfaction and job satisfaction. The MetLife study found that among employees who are highly satisfied with their benefits, 85% plan to be working for their current employer 18 months from now, compared to just 50% of those who are not satisfied with their benefits. In the coming decade, as economic and demographic changes affect the workforce and both employers' and employees' needs and wants, more employers will need to focus efforts on investing in human capital and retaining their workforce. All industries, in all company sizes and in every region of the country are likely to find themselves affected.

Small businesses should be encouraged to think through, not only what their workforce benefits needs are today, but also how they will attract and retain requisite talent to support growth plans for the future. MetLife's sixth annual Study of Employee Benefits Trends points to growing evidence that employees' benefits satisfaction will be an important strategy for success, and employers that can successfully optimize their benefits programs may find themselves more easily achieving their business objectives.

Ronald S. Leopold, MD, MBA, MPH
VP and National Medical Director
MetLife Institutional Business
Email: rleopold@metlife.com

ABOUT THE AUTHOR: Ronald S. Leopold, MD, MBA, MPH, is vice president and national medical director of MetLife Institutional Business. He focuses on the future of work, health and benefits. Dr. Leopold is a board certified occupational medicine physician who holds a Masters in Business Administration from the Wharton School of Business, the University of Pennsylvania and a Masters in Public Health from Boston University. He is the author of *A Year in the Life of a Million American Workers*, an almanac of absence data that provides a comprehensive picture of one million American workers and their health conditions, illnesses and absence patterns over a one-year period. He is currently at work on his next book entitled, *The Benefits Edge: Honing the Competitive Value of Employee Benefits*.

Robert D. Bucci, CEBS
VP, Small Market Strategy
MetLife Employee Benefits Sales
Email: rbucci@metlife.com

ABOUT THE AUTHOR: Robert D. Bucci is vice president, small market strategy, for MetLife Employee Benefits Sales. In this role, he is responsible for the company's small market sales strategy and development. Bucci has worked in the insurance industry in advancing positions of responsibility for over 25 years. He holds a B.S. degree in Business Administration from Fairleigh Dickinson University and holds a Certified Employee Benefits Specialist designation.

MetLife information can be obtained at 1-800-MET-LIFE. MetLife's sixth annual Employee Benefits Trends Study referenced in this chapter can be obtained at whymetlife.com/trendspr along with a wealth of other related resources.

Health Savings Accounts
The Savior of Our Medical System?

Josh Patrick, CFP®, Principal
Stage 2 Planning Partners

We read on a regular basis that our health care system is in crisis. Costs are out of control and quality is declining. Utilization rates are up and high-tech medical expenses are spiraling out of control. Not to mention, the cost of malpractice insurance has reached the point where some doctors are deciding to practice without any at all.

Some of us have been forced to ask employees to pay a significant portion of their own health coverage. In fact, many companies are only able to cover 50% of the expenses in a typical family's insurance plan, if that. With 15-30% annual increases in the cost of health insurance, many of us will have no choice but to continue decreasing the amount we pay toward our employee's health care coverage.

John Aardvark has a problem. He just received the renewal for his employee's health care policy and, to his displeasure, found it included a 15% increase in costs, to take effect in 30 days. This was the third year in a row that health care costs had increased by a rate that was at least three times that of inflation.

Health insurance is an extremely important and costly part of your benefit package. We all know that we can't afford to continue paying for dramatic increases in our health care. If you live in states that have moved toward a single payer system, you probably have seen no improvements in efficiencies. In fact, you may have seen just the opposite. With the additional cost for government-provided care shifting to the private sector, (in the end it only covers 50-75% of the true expenses) our health care systems have become even more bloated.

John talked with his medical insurance broker, asking why the insurance system rewards people who utilize the system a lot and penalizes those who only use it a little. John concluded that, while Americans are good at controlling costs in many parts of their lives, they aren't very good at controlling health care expenses. "Our system is completely upside-down because no one has any real financial responsibility when it comes to paying for his or her health care," he said.

John's broker informed him of a new type of health insurance program that puts financial responsibility on the side of the insured and gives them an incentive to use the system only when it is truly needed. It's called a Health Savings Account (HSA).

Created in Congress to allow high-deductible medical plans to have a savings component attached to them, the Health Savings Account requires that participants have a high-deductible policy in place of at least $2,500 for a single person and $4,000 for a family plan. With this plan in place, they now have the opportunity to fund a special savings account — the HSA — that allows them to put money away to pay that deductible, on a tax-deductible basis.

So, if your employee has a single insurance plan and your cost is $225 per month, you (or they) would have the option of putting $2,800 in the HSA.

The Health Savings Account can be funded by either the employer or the employee or a combination of both.

The good news is, if money from the health savings account is not used, the employee can use it for retirement.

When comparing the cost of a high-deductible plan that includes a HSA to a fully insured plan, the costs are usually about the same. For example, if you were to fund a HSA with the maximum contribution, the cost for a single policy with a high deductible of $2,500 would be $208.33 per month (or $2,500 for the year). When you combine this with the cost of the health insurance cost of $225 per month, the total health care bill would be $433.33 per month. This is comparable to the cost of a fully insured plan.

The true benefit is that if the insured doesn't spend the entire $2,500 on health care-related expenses they are able to apply the left over amount toward their own retirement. This being the case, it now makes sense for employees to shop for the best deal they can get on health care because every dollar they save they get to keep.

John liked the idea of this plan, but he saw no advantage to switching because he wouldn't be saving any money. He also saw a lot of complications in getting the plan off the ground.

It's true that a high-deductible HSA plan will cost approximately the same as a fully insured plan during its first year of operation. However, the increase in cost over time should be less than a fully insured plan and the difference in the amount of price increases will help to control your overall health benefit expenses.

As with all changes, especially those that are complicated, you will need to have a well-thought-out strategy for implementing the new plan. It's important for your employees to understand that by paying attention to their health costs, they will have a chance to reap major benefits for their own retirement.

John was ready to implement the plan, but he didn't know what needed to be done in order to introduce it. He also needed to have a strategy in place to help employees pay deductibles should they have high health costs during the first year the plan is in place. John asked his health insurance broker for suggestions on implementing the plan so his employees could easily see the benefits.

The cost for John's present plan is $400 per month for a single participants and $900 per month for married participants. John's company pays the full cost for only the single policy. This means that people who are married have to contribute $500 per month toward their total medical insurance expenses.

John and his broker decided that they would freeze the cost while changing to the new plan. This means the plan would work in the following manner:

Single Insurance Cost Company Paid $250.00

Monthly Health Savings Deposit Company Paid $150.00

Monthly Health Savings Deposit Employee Paid $33.33

Family Insurance Employee Paid $475.00

Family Insurance Company Paid $25.00

Monthly Health Savings Account Company Paid $375.00

When introducing the plan to employees, John announced that those who had been with the company for more than three years would be given an advance on the company's health savings deposits should they or their family need health care deductible coverage and the funds were not yet available in their accounts.

John decided it was important for the company to fund the majority of the HSA to make sure money was available for deductible expenses. He was concerned that, if he let his employees make this decision, many of them would not fund the savings accounts and would not have funds available when needed.

John also realized that it requires a significant amount of training and education for employees to understand the plan and how they can start controlling their own health care costs. He decided to present a case study to them at monthly meetings to talk about how the plan works. He knew people would relate to these real world stories and better understand the HSA and the benefits it provides to them.

John feels his company is well on its way toward controlling its long-term health care costs. He knows his employees will be better stewards of their health care dollars now that they have a direct interest in how those dollars are spent.

◆◆◆

3. 401(k)s and Related Retirement Plans

Michael J. Searcy, ChFC, CFP®, AIFA®
Searcy Financial Services, Inc.

The first step in creating the right employer-sponsored retirement plan, or in reviewing an existing plan, is to clarify what you consider to be a successful retirement plan. Too often, plans are set up without a clear vision — ultimately unraveling because of service issues, fees, investment performance expectations, or other issues. This chapter is designed to help you understand what issues must be addressed as you look to develop and manage a successful plan. It will also provide you with information on what tools are available to help you achieve your vision of success.

Defining Success

Success depends on an employer's objectives when establishing a retirement plan. It depends on the sponsor's understanding of the plan, and the amount of work required from the company's owner or HR personnel to manage the plan. Success also depends a great deal on how much the employees understand the benefits provided to them. Do employees feel they can take advantage of the benefits? Do they feel their plan is providing the resources to help prepare them for retirement?

As you look to define your vision of plan success, documenting the goals and objectives of your plan is a starting point, moving you toward your desired outcome in offering an employer-sponsored plan.

Types of Retirement Plans

There are several different types of retirement plans for small businesses. You will need to evaluate which plan is most likely to help you achieve your retirement plan goals. Some of the things to consider when selecting a plan include:

- What goals do you have in offering a retirement plan?
- What benefits are important to the company?
- What level of service do you expect from your plan provider?
- What kind of plan will the employees understand and appreciate?
- What regulations will govern the retirement plan?
- How much money can be set aside each year in the plan?
- What investment options do you want to have available to you in the plan? (These options can include mutual funds, professionally managed accounts, company stock and other options.)

Most small business retirement plans are either defined benefit plans or defined contribution plans. Defined benefit plans promise a specified benefit at retirement (for example, $100 a month beginning at retirement). The amount of the benefit is often based on several factors including age, and a fixed percentage of salary multiplied by the number of years the employee worked for the employer offering the plan. Employer contributions to the plan must be sufficient to fund the promised benefit.

Defined contribution plans, on the other hand, do not promise a specific amount of benefit at retirement. In these plans, employees or their employer (or both) contribute to employees' individual accounts under the plan, sometimes at a fixed rate (for example, 4% of salary annually) and sometimes at a variable rate based upon profits earned by the company. Normally, the variable portion is called a profit sharing plan which can be a stand-alone plan or added to a 401(k) plan.

While a small business may use any number of plan types to meet their needs, the most common retirement plans in use are SIMPLE (Savings Incentive

Match Plan for Employees), SEPs (Simplified Employee Pension Plan), 401(k), and payroll deduction IRAs (Individual Retirement Account). All retirement plans have important tax, business, and other implications for employers and employees. Therefore, you may want to discuss any retirement savings plan with a tax or financial advisor before selecting a plan for your business.

SIMPLE plans are easy to set up: simply fill out a short form to establish a plan and ensure that IRA accounts are set up for each employee. A SIMPLE plan allows employees to contribute a percentage of their salary from each paycheck and to have their employer contribute as well. Employees are 100% vested in contributions, decide how and where the money will be invested, and keep their IRA accounts when they leave the company.

> Even if an employer does not want to adopt a retirement plan, employees can save through payroll deduction.

A SEP allows employers to set up a type of individual retirement account for themselves and their employees. Employers must contribute a uniform percentage of their salary for each employee, although they do not have to make contributions every year. SEPs have low start-up and operating costs and can be established using a short form. Since you decide how much to put into a SEP each year, this plan offers you some flexibility when business conditions vary.

Even if an employer does not want to adopt a retirement plan, employees can save through payroll deduction, a simple and direct way for eligible employees to contribute to an IRA. In this type of arrangement, the decision about when and how much to contribute to the IRA is always made by the employee.

401(k) Plans

401(k) plans have become a widely-accepted retirement savings vehicle for small businesses. By year-end 2007, 401(k) plan assets had grown to more than $3 trillion.[1] According to the Hewitt Associates *2007 Trends and Experiences in 401(k) Plans* survey, almost two-thirds of employers (65%) report that the 401(k) plan is the primary retirement savings vehicle of the employees they cover.[2] Because of the popularity of this type of retirement plan, the

---

1 Insurance Information Institute, www.iii.org
2 "Survey Highlights: Trends and Experience in 401(k) Plans in 2007," Hewitt Knowledge Center: Articles & Reports, Hewitt Associates, LLC, Nov. 2007 <http://www.hewittassociates.com/Intl/NA/en-US/KnowledgeCenter/ArticlesReports/ArticleDetail. aspx?cid=4519>

remainder of this chapter will focus on 401(k) options, planning tools, and the responsibility of the plan sponsor in running a successful 401(k) plan.

Offering a 401(k) plan can be one of the most challenging, yet satisfying, decisions an employer can make. Both the employees participating in the plan and the employer benefit when a well-designed 401(k) plan is in place. Small business owners sponsor 401(k) plans for a variety of reasons, some of which include:

- Attracting and retaining talented employees.

- Allowing employees to decide how much to contribute to their accounts on a before-tax basis.

- Contributing to their employees' accounts, while simultaneously qualifying for a tax deduction.

- Offering benefits to both rank-and-file employees as well as the owners/managers.

- Providing employees with a retirement vehicle, in which contributed monies may grow through investments in stocks, mutual funds, money market funds and other investments.

- Presenting employees with a tax-deferred retirement savings opportunity.

- Easing administration burdens, since some employees may take their benefits with them when they leave the company.

Types of 401(k) Plans

There are many practical benefits of sponsoring a 401(k) plan for your employees, as well as many options in setting up the plan. Under the 401(k) umbrella, there are four main types of plans available to small business owners: *traditional, Safe Harbor, SIMPLE,* and *Roth* 401(k) plans. For self-employed business owners who have no other employees but themselves, there is also a *Solo* 401(k).

- A *traditional* 401(k) plan is available to employers of any size and offers the most flexibility of the four types of plans. You can add it to the mix of benefits you offer your employees, since it can be combined with any number of different retirement plans. This plan is subject to annual discrimination testing in order to ensure that benefits for the rank-and-file employees are proportionate to benefits for the owners/

managers. Investments can be directed by either the employer/trustee or the individual participant, depending on the plan design.

- A *Safe Harbor* 401(k) is similar in many ways to the traditional 401(k). One of the differences is that a Safe Harbor plan is not subject to many of the complex tax rules or discrimination testing associated with the traditional plan. Like a traditional 401(k), it is available to employers of any size, can be combined with other retirement plans and the investments can be directed by either the employer/trustee or the individual participants. Under the Pension Protection Act of 2006, there are three new "automatics" that offer Safe Harbor status. Each of these use the power of "inertia" to work for the benefit of employees because they are automatically saving for their retirement; only by affirmatively filing an election can they opt out of the default settings.

  > **Automatic enrollment:** The plan automatically enrolls employees by default and at a default contribution rate. Automatic enrollment radically increases employee participation rates, while simultaneously reducing potential liability risks for the employer.

  > **Automatic default into qualified default investment alternatives (QDIA):** The plan automatically invests an employee's 401(k) contributions into default investments, including maturity or age-based funds, risk-based lifestyle or balanced funds, or managed accounts.

  > **Automatic deferral increases:** The plan automatically starts employees at a deferral rate (typically 3% or 4%) and increases those rates up to as much as 10-15% of their compensation on a periodic basis.

- The *SIMPLE* 401(k) was created so that small businesses could have a cost-efficient way to offer retirement benefits to their employees. This plan is available to employers with 100 or fewer employees who received at least $5,000 in compensation from the employer in the previous year. Unlike other types of 401(k) plans, employees covered under a SIMPLE plan cannot participate in any other retirement plans offered by the employer and investment selection is directed by the individual participant.

- *Roth* 401(k) plans are hybrid retirement plans that combine characteristics of a traditional 401(k) and a Roth IRA. These types of plans allow employees to treat part or all of their contributions (deducted from their paychecks on an after-tax basis) as Roth contributions. In other words, they can use after-tax dollars to fund their Roth 401(k) and the growth on those contributions is not subject to income tax when the money is withdrawn. Other than this feature, Roth 401(k) plans operate much like traditional plans.

Employee Participation

All plans should include a blend of rank-and-file employees, as well as owners/managers. However, employees may be excluded from participation in the plan if they are under the age of 21, have not completed one year of service, and/or are covered by a collective bargaining agreement that does not provide for participation in the plan. Employees cannot be randomly excluded from the plan if they meet enrollment eligibility.

Contributions

Typically, there are two types of 401(k) contributions: employee contributions and employer contributions. With the exception of Roth 401(k) plans, employees can contribute to their accounts using pre-tax dollars, thereby lowering their taxable income. Employee contributions, usually accomplished through salary deferrals, are restricted to contribution limits dictated by current tax law. Current contribution limits can be found at the Internal Revenue Service website, www.irs.gov.

Depending on the type of 401(k) plan they have chosen to implement, small business owners have many options in deciding how much (if any) they will contribute to their employees' accounts. With *traditional* 401(k) plans, they can contribute a percentage of each employee's compensation, regardless of whether the employee makes a salary deferral into his or her own account. This is known as a nonelective contribution and employers have the flexibility of changing this amount each year, depending on business conditions and climate. The other option is to match the amount their employees decide to contribute (within the limits of current laws).

With a *Safe Harbor* 401(k) plan, employer contribution requirements are less flexible, since the employer must make either nonelective contributions or matching contributions, regardless of business conditions. Employer contributions must fall under the following guidelines:

- A nonelective contribution equal to 3% of each eligible employee's compensation, even if the employee does not contribute anything on their own behalf.

- A dollar-for-dollar match of up to 4% of employee compensation. Because it is a "matching" contribution, employees who are not contributing their own money to their accounts would not receive a matching contribution from the employer.

- A dollar-for-dollar match for the first 3% deferred by each non-highly compensated employee, and an additional 50% of the next 2% deferred.

SIMPLE 401(k) plans are limited to two options. The employer can make a nonelective contribution equal to 2% of employee compensation, or the employer can match each eligible employee's contribution dollar-for-dollar up to 3% of compensation.

Roth 401(k) plans have another layer of requirements to further complicate matters. Any contributions the employer makes toward the employee's Roth 401(k) must be deposited into a traditional 401(k) account using pre-tax dollars. In essence, employees have both a Roth 401(k) account (for employee contributions) and a traditional 401(k) account (for employer contributions). Other than this, the same employer contribution guidelines as the traditional 401(k) plans apply.

Vesting

With all 401(k) plans, employee salary deferrals are immediately 100% vested. In other words, the money that employees have contributed to their account cannot be forfeited. When employees leave the company, they are entitled to their contributions, plus any investment gains (or losses) on those deferrals.

Depending on the type of 401(k) plan you decide to implement, there are different rules regarding the vesting of employer contributions. For *Safe Harbor* or *SIMPLE* 401(k) plans, all employer contributions are immediately 100% vested, regardless of length of employment. For **traditional** and **Roth** 401(k) plans, employer contributions can be subject to a vesting schedule, depending on how the plan is designed. For example, if the plan dictates that employer contributions are 100% vested after four years, then employees are entitled to 100% of the employer contributions (plus any investment gains or losses) after four years of employment. Regardless, all matching contributions must be fully vested after a maximum six years of service.

Investing

Unless you have a *SIMPLE* 401(k) plan, one decision you will need to make in designing your plan is whether to permit your employees to direct the investments in their accounts. *Traditional, Safe Harbor* and *Roth* 401(k) plans all have the option of participant-directed or employer/trustee-directed investments.

In addition, you will need to select either a "closed architecture" or "open architecture" platform. Simply put, this refers to the availability of investment options within the plan. Typically, a plan has a "closed architecture" platform if it is offered through an insurance company or mutual fund family. Participants are limited to a pre-selected number of mutual funds (or insurance product sub-accounts) as investment options, or the plan offers choices of mutual funds that are labeled B, C, T, or R shares.

Conversely, a platform is considered "open architecture" if the plan sponsor has access to the entire universe of funds that are available through the plan's custodian.[3] There are clear advantages of an "open architecture" platform. One of the biggest advantages is the ability for the plan sponsor to access a more diverse selection of funds.[4] With this arrangement, participants have the ability to shift investment strategies, rotate sectors and further diversify, while utilizing a variety of share classes (i.e. no-load or low-cost index funds).

Plan Fees and Expenses

In order to ensure that plan expenses are reasonable, it is essential that small business owners have a full understanding of the fees and expenses associated with their 401(k) plan. Unfortunately, 401(k) plans are notorious for hidden fees and expenses; many employers do not know that they and/or their employees are needlessly paying an annual additional one percent to two percent directly out of their retirement accounts. Over time, these unnecessary fees could reduce a retirement nest egg by several thousands of dollars.

While a plan does not necessarily need to be the least expensive available, small business owners who sponsor a 401(k) plan for their employees should be able to show documentation for the decisions they have made regarding provider and investment selection—including a process to ensure expenses

---

3 A custodian is a financial institution that has the legal responsibility for a customer's securities. This implies management as well as safekeeping (examples: TD Ameritrade, Charles Schwab, and Fidelity).
4 It is important to note that while a plan could have an "open architecture" platform, the plan's third-party administrator may limit the investment options to a select group of funds to help control costs.

paid are not excessive when compared to similar options. Fees and expenses surrounding 401(k) plans generally fall into three categories:

1. Plan administration fees: Expenses incurred by the daily operation of the plan (i.e. record keeping, accounting, legal and trustee services).

2. Investment fees: Expenses associated with the management of the plan's investments. These fees most likely represent the bulk of the plan's expenses.

3. Individual service fees: Fees associated with optional features offered by the plan.

Whether you are setting up a new plan or looking to change an existing one, it is important to evaluate the fees of all potential service providers to verify that the providers you select are competitively priced, based on the needs of the plan.

The Minimum Standards

Federal law sets minimum standards for pension plans in the private sector (this includes 401(k) plans and other retirement plans offered by businesses for the benefit of their employees). ERISA (Employee Retirement Income Security Act of 1974) protects the assets of millions of Americans, helping ensure that funds placed in retirement plans during the employees' working lives will be available when they retire. It is important to note that ERISA does not require any employer to establish a retirement plan; it requires only that those who have chosen to establish plans meet some minimum standards. Specifically, ERISA does the following:

- Requires plans to provide participants with information about the plan, including important information about plan features and funding.

- Sets minimum standards for participation, vesting, benefit accrual and funding.

- Requires accountability of plan fiduciaries, who may be responsible for restoring losses to the plan if they do not follow the principles of conduct.

- Gives participants the right to sue for benefits and breaches of fiduciary duty.

- Guarantees payment of certain benefits if a defined benefit plan is terminated through a federally chartered corporation, known as the Pension Benefit Guarantee Corporation.

The Significance of Being a Fiduciary

The term "fiduciary" is not often tossed around in everyday conversation, but if you are considering offering a retirement plan to your employees, you must become familiar with its meaning, responsibilities, and implications. ERISA generally defines a fiduciary as anyone who exercises discretionary authority or control over a plan's management or assets, including anyone who provides investment advice to the plan. By definition, employers who sponsor a retirement plan for the benefit of their employees are *always* considered fiduciaries.

According to the U.S. Department of Labor, the agency responsible for enforcing the provisions of ERISA, fiduciaries have important responsibilities and are subject to standards of conduct because they act on behalf of participants in the retirement plan, as well as their beneficiaries. These responsibilities include:

- Acting solely in the interest of plan participants (and their beneficiaries), with the exclusive purpose of providing benefits to them.

- Carrying out their duties prudently.

- Following the plan documents (unless inconsistent with ERISA).

- Diversifying plan investments.

- Paying only reasonable plan expenses.

The implication for a small business owner who chooses to sponsor a retirement plan for the benefit of their employees is quite weighty. It cannot be stressed enough that:

*Plan fiduciaries can be held **personally** liable for the retirement plans they oversee.*

Often, employers shop for retirement plans as they would for any other product or service. They fail to take into account their fiduciary responsibility. However, with their personal assets on the line, the foremost question in the mind of a business owner should be, "How can I best satisfy my legal obligations as a fiduciary, while selecting a plan that's right for my employees?"

Higher Standards

In essence, ERISA (in combination with case law and regulatory opinion letters) provides the framework of sponsoring and running a retirement plan. While it gives employers the principles to follow, it does not provide details on how to follow them.

This is where Fiduciary360 can help. Fiduciary360 is an organization with a mission to help fiduciaries to fulfill their responsibilities. By laying out specific standards and steps to follow, they answer the "how" questions that ERISA neglects. For example, fiduciary legislation clearly requires that a due diligence process be followed in selecting an investment option; it does not define what constitutes a minimum due diligence process. Fiduciary360 combines the minimum requirements of pertinent legislation with industry best practices to ensure that any person in the position of having fiduciary responsibility can be certain they are meeting their obligations when they follow the process.

The **Prudent Practices** Handbook written by the Foundation for Fiduciary Studies (a division of Fiduciary360) defines seven standards to guide fiduciaries as they carry out their duties:[5]

- Know standards, laws and trust provisions.

- Diversify assets to specific risk/return profile of client.

- Prepare an investment policy statement.

- Use "prudent experts" (money managers) and document due diligence.

- Control and account for investment expenses.

- Monitor the activities of "prudent experts."

- Avoid conflicts of interest and prohibited transactions.

These higher standards create a solid foundation designed to guide fiduciaries in meeting their responsilibities.

The Benefits of Higher Standards

As fiduciaries, business owners sponsoring a 401(k) plan have a solemn responsibility to protect the interests of their employees. In a time when small business owners must make difficult decisions about cutting corners, it might seem easiest to simply comply with the minimum standards as set forth in ERISA. However, in today's litigious society, it makes good sense for fiduciaries to do everything in their power to limit

---

5 Fiduciary360, Prudent Practices for Investment Advisors (Sewickley, PA: Fiduciary360, 2006) 7.

their liablity exposure.

Fiduciaries, in particular, are exposed to legal and practical scrutiny coming from multiple directions for various reasons. Fiduciary liability arises when a process is not defined and/or inconsistently applied. The most important thing to remember is that the fiduciary plan sponsor must follow a prudent process. Plan sponsors are not to be judged by the results they obtain. Instead, the steps leading to a plan's success or failure serve to measure plan sponsor performance. In this sense, it's not whether you win or lose. It's how you play the game.

Beyond limiting your liability exposure, following the higher standards can result in a more efficient 401(k) plan due to:

- Greater ease of administration.
- Full understanding of requirements.
- Simplified management.
- Assistance with fiduciary obligations.
- Successful compliance tests.
- Competitive investment returns.
- High participation and contribution rates.
- Employees who understand and appreciate benefits.

Getting Help

The average small business owner is in a tough position. On one hand, he or she needs to offer competitive benefit packages, including retirement plans, to attract and retain high-quality employees. However, by doing so, a business owner must take on the full mantle of fiduciary liability risk. For most business owners, looking for a financial advisor who can help in fulfilling their responsibilities as a fiduciary is a smart decision.

Even though a business owner may seek help and advice, it is important to note that an employer can never "give away" fiduciary responsibility; it is impossible to outsource the full weight of the responsibility to someone else. However, employers can hire a financial advisor who will share in their obligations by virtually eliminating the fiduciary responsibility (and liability) for the selection and monitoring of plan investment options. It is wise to look for an investment advisor who will act as a fiduciary in the management of plan assets. Unfortunately, there are few investment advisors who are willing to do so, and few who will acknowledge their fiduciary role in writing.

In order to find the kind of advisor who will help you carry out your fiduciary responsibilities as a plan sponsor, look for an advisor who adheres to the Global Fiduciary Standards of Excellence, as defined by Fiduciary360. Specifically, look for an advisor with an AIFA® designation (i.e. Accredited Investment Fiduciary Analyst™). This designation, awarded by the Center for Fiduciary Studies, in association with the Joseph M. Katz Graduate School of Business at the University of Pittsburg, focuses on all the components of a comprehensive investment process, related fiduciary standards of care, and a commitment to excellence. Advisors with this designation have completed the initial training programs and annual continuing education requirements, and have pledged to abide by a code of ethics. For employers seeking guidance, an advisor with this training is a good place to start.

> For most business owners, looking for a financial advisor who can help in fulfilling their responsibilities as a fiduciary is a smart decision.

Making the Right Choice

Unless you have clearly defined a vision of success for your plan, it is difficult to know whether or not you have a successful retirement plan in place. Start by considering these questions:

- What goals do you have in offering a retirement plan?
  - ▶ Attract new employees?
  - ▶ Retain employees?
  - ▶ Benefit key employees?
  - ▶ Allow employee pre-tax retirement savings?
  - ▶ Accumulate substantial retirement income for owner(s)?
- What level of service do you expect?
- Do you feel your employees understand and appreciate the benefit offered in the retirement plan?

Once you have defined objectives, you can move forward to confidently face the numerous options available, ultimately choosing a plan and advisor that will meet your needs and help you achieve your goals.

Michael J. Searcy, ChFC, CFP®, AIFA®, President
Searcy Financial Services, Inc.
13220 Metcalf Avenue, Ste. 360
Overland Park, KS 66213
Tel: 913.814.3800
Email: Mike@SearcyFinancial.com
http://www.SearcyFinancial.com

ABOUT THE AUTHOR: Michael J. Searcy, ChFC, CFP®, AIFA®, is an Accredited Investment Fiduciary Analyst™ designee and President of Searcy Financial Services, Inc., an independent, financial planning and wealth management firm registered with the SEC. With more than 30 years of experience, Michael has been featured as a noted author and speaker in numerous local and national publications. His firm has been included as one of the "Top Wealth Managers" in the nation by *Wealth Manager Magazine,* as well as one of "The Most Dependable™ Wealth Managers in the Central U.S." in *Forbes® Magazine,* as selected by Goldline Research. Michael's priority is to offer his clients excellent service, timely information and quality advice. He specializes in helping small business owners navigate through a myriad of decisions and issues including: succession planning, partnership buy-ins or buy-outs, 401(k) plan solutions and retirement plans. His firm utilizes a team approach to deliver the most accurate information available, while making available the highest quality of services and products on an open-architected platform, so his clients' choices are not limited. As a Registered Investment Advisor, his firm is held to the highest ethical standards in the financial services industry, with the fiduciary requirement to put their clients' interests first.

Michael would like to thank his staff, especially Kristin Fillingham, Jessica Maldonado, and Randy Schaller for their contributions to the creation and development of this chapter.

Success Elements for Hiring and Retention

Rafael Pastor, Chairman of the Board and CEO
Vistage International

The Vistage CEO Confidence Index, a quarterly survey of CEOs of small to mid-size businesses, consistently finds that the top CEO concern is retaining and recruiting talent. Growth and innovation depend on motivated, talented people working well together. Simply put, a businesses' most valuable asset is its employees.

The key to personnel success is to have a staffing system that maps out a consistent process for how your company recruits, screens, interviews, evaluates and hires new employees. A well-designed staffing system has three bottom-line benefits: 1) It optimizes your resources; 2) It reduces risk and uncertainty in the hiring process; and 3) It increases not only your odds of hiring the right person, but also the likelihood of a cohesive and collaborative culture in your company. Below are the key elements of a solid staffing system.

The Performance-Based Job Profile

It's imperative to have an objective set of criteria that spells out the essential activities a person must perform and the outcomes he or she must deliver. The best way to predict future job success is to uncover examples of past performance using a performance-based job profile. Build each job profile around objective, quantifiable, measurable criteria that includes three to five of the most important outcomes a person needs to deliver, and the skills and characteristics the person needs to get the job done, stated in specific terms of knowledge, abilities and experience. Review and update job profiles at least once a year. Companies with rapid growth curves may need to update every three to six months. A staffing system built around performance-based criteria allows hiring managers to reduce personal bias and focus on matching the right candidate to the specific job.

Recruiting

To recruit successfully, you need to get the word out to as many people as you can that you're looking for talent. The key is to use multiple outreach tools that work concurrently. Here are some ideas: Encourage your employees to refer candidates with an employee-referral program that offers bonuses and rewards. Create compelling, opportunity-focused job ads that describe what the person needs to do, more than what skills they need to have, to broaden the pool of qualified candidates. Allow multiple inflow avenues, such as employee, customer and vendor referrals, temps-to-perms, interns, and trade shows/conventions. Consider short-term consulting contracts at the senior level and look into outsourcing and job sharing. Read the papers for news of layoffs, mergers and acquisitions and companies whose stock price is declining. And never stop recruiting, even when you don't have any job openings.

Screening

Properly screening résumés enables you to narrow the pool of candidates to a manageable size with a minimum of time and effort. Look for achievements that closely correlate to the job at hand, and use résumés to screen in rather than screen out. The last thing you want to do is inadvertently weed out great candidates. Never bring someone in for an interview without an initial phone screen. The 10 to 15 minutes you spend up front with candidates can save hours of time later.

Interviewing

A structured interview uses a prepared list of questions designed to uncover information related to the job profile. This process keeps the hiring manager focused on gathering examples of past performance, prevents the candidate from taking control of the interview, reduces subjectivity and personal bias in the process, and provides an objective methodology for evaluating candidates.

The more examples of past performance you can find that match the job profile, the more you can make objective hiring decisions. During the interview, avoid opinion-, credential- or experience-based questions. Instead, ask behavior-based questions that uncover an applicant's specific work-related experiences and their past job performance.

One question that I like to ask job candidates is this: Do you consider yourself lucky? If the candidate says "yes," I then ask for an example of their "luck." If they describe an opportunity that they creatively took advantage of, it indicates that this person can find the openings to make things happen, that he or she is a "doer" who can go beyond what's merely expected. I also like to ask what a person is reading and how they spend their leisure time. This helps me gauge the candidate's breadth of curiosity and areas of interest.

Additionally, when a candidate discusses their work at a past job using the term "we" (e.g., we launched a new product), I ask them to put it in terms of "I". I want to know what the candidate himself or herself actually did and is proud of.

Remember to check all references to verify or uncover information that might influence your decision. If it's an important hire, you, yourself, might speak with a prior boss and not delegate that to your HR person. Lastly, to improve the quality of your company's hiring decisions, have your hiring managers update their interviewing skills at least once a year.

Making the Decision

Rate candidates based on their past job performance. During the interview candidates should give recent examples of impactful behavior. Look for candidates who describe "but for" situations — an achievement that would not have happened at their prior company but for their involvement or role. What was it that this candidate did that made the difference?

Try to determine if the candidate exhibits quality behavior. Follow up with the candidate's references to verify his or her claims.

Use a quantifiable, measurable scoring system and evaluate candidates against your standard, not against each other. Also, consider using personality assessment tests on potential hires. These tests are specifically designed to uncover red flags and potentially serious issues.

If none of the candidates meet your standard, don't hire any of them. Instead, step back and reevaluate your job profile to make sure it is realistic. If so, go back to the recruiting process and start over again.

With a staffing system in place and benchmarks and standards established for each position in your company, you will gradually improve the level of talent in your workforce. The growth of your talent pool will help fuel the growth and innovativeness of your company.

The Importance of Employee Retention

Employee retention rates are a reflection of company morale. Happy, engaged employees are more productive, tend to make more sales and serve customers better. These employees stay at their jobs longer than unhappy ones, and they ultimately make more money for the company. Disgruntled, unengaged employees tend to generate more negative customer experiences. They are often disinterested in working toward company growth and other objectives and may even be subversive.

To have a positive impact on employee retention, CEOs must recognize some fundamentals about the current employment environment.

1. **Today's employees have more choices than ever.** "In the old days," says employee retention expert Nancy Ahlrichs, "you could make unbendable rules and treat everyone the same. Today's employees refuse to put up with it. If managers treat them unfairly, they will leave and find someone better to work for."

2. **Potential hires are ambassadors for your company.** Job candidates — whether they get hired or not — serve as unpaid ambassadors in the community for your company. Their experience with your hiring managers will determine whether their message casts your organization in a positive light. If enough candidates have a bad interview experience with your company, you may soon find that the "recruiting well" is poisoned.

3. **Different generations have different expectations and attitudes.** Generation X and Y workers may not envision spending their careers with one company, but they are innovative, creative and tech savvy. To retain them, offer them benefits that they see as valuable to maintaining their lifestyle, and adjust your management style to get the most from them. Companies can motivate and retain Gen Xers by offering career growth and advancement opportunities and personal acknowledgement. Progressive companies keep Gen Yers by offering them more flexible work schedules and venues, ongoing training, consistent feedback, and immediate rewards for jobs well done.

Managers are Critical in Retaining Employees

When it comes to retaining employees, great managers do key things with their employees. They foster:

- Upward career potential and mobility
- Participation in company growth
- Continuing training and education
- Recognition and reward for performance
- Flexibility with where and when they do their work

Showing this sort of respect for talent keeps employees engaged in their work. The single most powerful motivator for employees is not pay; it's the opportunity to work in an engaging job that offers plenty of challenge, learning and growth while allowing the individual to feel he or she is having an impact on something that's valuable. When these elements are in place, your top performers have fewer reasons to look for jobs elsewhere.

◆◆◆

4. Insurance Planning: Big Ideas for Small Business

John Ryan, CFP®

Ryan Insurance Strategy Consultants

I am a small business owner, and I am an insurance advisor. I have been both for the past 30 years. I have built a successful career by helping small business owners make good choices when selecting life insurance, disability insurance, and long-term care insurance plans. I will share with you my insights into the world of insurance and help you, the small business owner, make good choices and avoid the bad ones when shopping for insurance solutions for your family, business or estate.

Assuming that you have a basic understanding of life, disability and long-term care insurance, this chapter will concentrate on certain policy features, plan designs, and concepts that I believe are the most important and have the potential to give you the biggest return on your investment.

If you need to learn the basics, there are plenty of websites, including my own, that can quickly get you up to speed.

Here are just a few of the important questions I will address:

1. When should I buy term life vs. permanent (cash value) life insurance?

2. How do I determine how much I need and how long I need it?

3. Why are conversion options important when buying a term insurance policy?

4. How do I avoid worrying about my permanent life insurance policy performance?

5. How can I be sure I am getting the best possible insurance advice?

6. What disability plan makes the best sense for a newly self-employed business owner?

7. How do I overcome my objection to the price of disability insurance?

8. Is long-term care insurance something I should buy? If so, when and how much should I buy?

9. What plan policy designs considerations must I have and which ones can I do without when buying a life, disability or long-term care policy?

10. How much should I expect to pay for a competitive life, disability or long-term care insurance plan?

Before you buy life, disability, or long-term care insurance, you should have a formal plan that outlines why you need it, what type you need, how much you need, and how long you will need it. These are questions central to the discussion of insurance. I believe it is best to have an objective financial advisor prepare a comprehensive financial plan for a fee that includes answers to the above questions. This is the best way to start the process of insurance planning.

Life Insurance

Term Life Insurance — There are two basic types of policies. They are term insurance (no cash value) and permanent insurance (cash value). First let's talk about term insurance. This is the least expensive form of insurance! Policies can be programmed to last up to 30 years in five-year increments. Because of this, I believe you should buy term insurance when your need for protection is perceived to be 30 years or less. Term life is ideal for providing protection for income replacement, debt reduction, college funding and buy-sell agreements. However, when you buy term insurance you run the risk of wanting the insurance to last longer than originally planned. So, when you select a time frame like 15 years, you may want to be conservative and purchase a 20-year plan, just to be on the safe side. You can always reduce or cancel the insurance as your needs decrease.

Of course, if you do wish to extend the coverage, you can go shopping again for another term life plan and lock in coverage for another 10 or 15 years. The problem with this strategy is you may be in poor health and a new policy purchased later on may be cost-prohibitive or unavailable if you are uninsurable. That is why it is so important to purchase a term policy with a conversion option. A conversion option allows you to purchase a permanent policy without having to prove you are insurable. Insist that your policy have a conversion option for the full length of the premium guarantee period. For example, if you are age 47 and are purchasing a 20-year level premium term policy, make sure your conversion option is available through age 67. Important: Watch out, some policies terminate the conversion option prematurely so you cannot convert later.

> It's so important to purchase a term policy with a conversion option. A conversion option allows you to purchase a permanent policy without having to prove you are insurable.

Most term life proposals indicate at what age the conversion options terminate. If not, ask your agent to show you, in writing, through what age they are available. You can also review your conversion option rights once you receive your actual policy.

Suffice to say, a conversion option can save you thousands of dollars later on. Naturally, for all of your insurance needs you should purchase from a financially sound and reputable insurance company. Insist that your life insurance company (disability and long-term care companies, too) have a COMDEX rating of at least 80, preferably higher. A COMDEX rating is the percentile rank of a company based on their financial strength in relation to other insurance companies, and they rate insurance companies on a scale of 1-100. A rating of 85% means your company has financial strength greater than 85% of the industry.

Permanent Insurance — These policies cost more than four times as much as term, but have the potential of returning some of the additional cost to you in the form of cash surrender values. As the name implies, permanent insurance (i.e. Whole Life, Universal Life, and Variable Universal Life) were designed to provide permanent protection, meaning the rest of your life. They are used most often to fund life insurance trusts. If you can't use term insurance to solve your problem, then permanent insurance may be your only option. Be sure to blend as much term life as possible into your permanent policy design to create better values.

Whole Life (WL) — If you consider whole life, make sure you include a mutual company (dividend paying) in your analysis. Whole life policies are the most expensive, but generate greater cash values if the right company is selected.

Universal Life (UL) — This is the most popular type of permanent insurance sold today. UL is more flexible than whole life (i.e. you can change certain plan features later on) and can provide longer-term premiums and death benefit guarantees than whole life. Some UL policies, called Guaranteed Universal Life (GUL) can be purchased with guaranteed premiums and death benefits to age 120. These policies usually do not have long-term cash value accumulations because the buyer is less interested in cash value and more interested in the lower cost, fully guaranteed contract. Because of these guarantees, these policies have become the most popular choice among estate planning attorneys, CPAs, and trustees.

Variable Universal Life (VUL) — When structured properly, VUL policies can be a good choice for permanent needs. However, because the policy performance may be so closely correlated to the stock market, you would be wise to monitor the policy values every three years. Although there is greater potential for increased cash value and death benefits, the downside risk is also greater than with the fixed products previously described. Simply request a policy "in-force" illustration from the agent and compare it to the original sales illustration. This will help you spot problems with policy performance well before it is to late to avoid a significant increase in premium or a lapsed policy.

With cash value products, you should choose a company with a COMDEX rating of at least 90. And always seek a second opinion when you are considering a permanent life insurance policy. I see more mistakes made in this area than any other. Most have to do with suitability. Also be sure to consult your attorney for proper wording of all ownership and beneficiary designations on life insurance contracts.

Insurance advisors may recommend you buy permanent insurance now because term life insurance becomes too expensive later on. Although it is true that term rates will be higher after the premium guarantee expires, you do have a few choices at that time.

a. You may find you no longer need or want protection after the term period expires, in which case you don't have a need for permanent (cash value) insurance or,

b. You may be healthy enough at the end of the term period to medically qualify for a new, reasonably priced term policy and extend your coverage for another 10 to 15 years, or

c. If you are not healthy enough to repurchase at that time, you can convert your term life policy to a permanent policy without evidence of insurability. In fact, you will receive the same health rating you received when you first purchased your term policy. This assumes, of course, that your term policy has a good conversion option available to you at that time. Make sure of this when purchasing a term policy. (I suggest you go to my website and read the report I wrote on conversion options.)

Some insurance advisors may persist, though, stating, "Yes, this is true, but the cost of permanent insurance at age 75 will be four times that of a permanent policy today, so it is less expensive in the long run (to age 95) to buy permanent insurance now."

Although it is true that permanent insurance will be four times more expensive at age 75 than at age 45, think about all the money you saved in the form of lower premiums for the first 30 years. These savings can be used to cover the higher cost of permanent insurance later on. To illustrate my point, let's look at Chart #1 on page 58:

Any financial advisor would tell you not to focus on total premiums paid, but on the present value of those payments. In other words, how much money would you have to have in the bank today to pay for all future premiums, assuming you earned 5% after-tax on your money and made those payments for 50 years as illustrated. Clearly, it doesn't cost more to buy term life now, you can "wait and see" if you will want permanent protection later. If you do, convert to a permanent policy then.

Please note, these calculations don't take into account the potential cash value accumulation of the permanent policy you may buy now. These accumulations may be used in the future to reduce premium payments or returned

Chart #1: The Wait-and-See Approach to Buying Permanent Life Insurance

	MALE		FEMALE	
	ANNUAL PREMIUMS		ANNUAL PREMIUMS	
	Term Life W/Conversion Option	Permanent Life Insurance	Term Life W/Conversion Option	Permanent Life Insurance
Years 1-30	$1,880	$7,000	$1,400	$5,500
Years 31-50	$30,000	$7,000	$2,000	$5,500
Total Premiums Paid to Age 95	$654,000	$350,000	$442,000	$275,000
Present Value of Total Premium @ 5%	$115,535	$128,000	$79,500	$100,000

***All quotes assume a $1,000,000 policy, preferred health, non-smoker.

to you in the form of cash withdrawals, or upon surrender of your policy. This should be taken into account when performing a detailed present value calculation on the specific policy you may be considering. But keep in mind, although you don't have a "cash value build-up" when you buy the term life policy, it is assumed you are investing the premium savings ($5,120/Yr for the male and $4,120/Yr for the female from our previous illustration) over the 30-year period. You are, in essence, creating your own cash value, but outside of the policy, not within. And you can probably outperform the policy values with the help of a good financial advisor.

Disability Insurance

Most business owners must have disability insurance, but I am often alarmed at how many do not. They may not be aware of how a slight reduction in their ability to work can lead to a great loss of earnings.

Let me illustrate my point. This business owner is well and working with the following revenue.

$30,000/mo gross revenue

- $15,000/mo business expenses

$15,000/mo net income to owner

Now assume the business revenue decreases by 25% because the owner's capabilities at work have been reduced due to a stamina or dexterity problem. Look at what happens to the owner's net income, especially when expenses are roughly the same.

$22,500/mo gross revenue

- $13,500/mo business expenses

$ 9,000/mo net income to owner

This slight reduction in production leads to a significant (40%) loss of income to the owner. For a business with an overhead factor greater than 50%, which most businesses have, the results will be even more devastating to the owner.

Knowing how vulnerable they are to a reduction of income, why do so many business owners not purchase adequate coverage? The answer is the perceived high cost of coverage.

The reason I say "perceived high cost of coverage" is because agents often recommend the wrong policy or policy design to the business owner. This problem is even worse when the owner is in the first few years of developing his or her business and every dime counts. Here are some suggestions that may help you get adequate disability coverage now with the thought of upgrading later on.

> Most business owners must have disability insurance, but I am often alarmed at how many do not. They may not be aware of how a slight reduction in their ability to work can lead to a great loss of earnings.

1. If you have three or more employees in your company, you can get guaranteed issue group Long-Term Disability (LTD) coverage from most major LTD insurance providers. The cost is 20% of an individual policy and no one can be turned down for health reasons. This is a great employee benefit as well, helping to attract and retain employees.

2. Once your annual income exceeds $75,000, consider purchasing an individual disability policy as a supplement. There are a number of reasons why this makes sense, but the most obvious are the increase in tax-free benefits and better definitions of disability found in individual policies.

3. When buying an individual policy for the first time, consider a plan design that is similar to group LTD. This would mean getting a policy with the following features:

a. Guaranteed Renewable (GR) instead of Non-Cancelable (NC)

GR policies are 30% less expensive than NC policies. The difference is GR policies do not have a long-term price guarantee. You can upgrade to a NC policy later when your income increases.

b. Integrate policy benefits with social security and worker compensation benefits. (Don't do this if you have a group LTD because group LTD already offsets with benefits from the government and you don't want to double offset). Integrating a policy will reduce policy premium benefits by 10%. Integrating means your policy will reduce its benefits, dollar-for-dollar, by what you receive from the government. There is a limit on how much your benefits will reduce. If you do not receive government benefits, your policy benefits will not be reduced.

c. Hold off on buying a cost-of-living adjustment rider. This will reduce costs by as much as 30%. This feature should be added as soon as cash flow permits because policy benefits, without this option, will only be worth half their value in 24 years, assuming a 3% inflation rate.

4. For female business owners only: You may be able to create a 30% discount in premium by structuring your policy under a qualified sick pay plan arrangement. (See your agent to determine your eligibility.)

Starting with a basic plan may be your best option. Be sure to consider upgrading over the next three to five years.

I suggest you purchase the following basic features immediately:

1. Modified own-occupation definition of disability: This definition means you will receive full benefits if you are sick or hurt and can't work in your own occupation and you choose not to work. If you choose to work, you still receive full benefits until your income exceeds 20% of your pre-disability earnings. If your income exceeds 20% of your pre-disability earnings, you will receive a percentage of your monthly benefit equal to your percent loss of earnings (i.e. 50% loss of earnings times monthly benefit equals benefit paid). The key to this definition is that it is built into most individual policies at no additional cost, pays full benefits if you choose not to work once disabled, and even if you do return to work and earn income, the policy still pays partial (residual) benefits.

2. Residual disability benefits: These are partial disability benefits and should be included in your policy. As illustrated earlier, even partial disability can lead to a great loss of net income.

3. Future insurability options: These options allow you to purchase more coverage in the future without having to prove insurability. These are invaluable and you should purchase the maximum amount of options available to cover your projected income growth. These options must be used by a certain age, usually 50, 55, or even age 60 with some policies.

Don't allow all the confusion concerning features and definitions to get in the way of making a prudent decision. Keep it simple. I can illustrate my point with the Job A vs. Job B scenario I like so much. I know this is an over-simplification, but bear with me for a moment.

Assume you walked into a potential employer's office and she said they were going to make you the following offer:

Job "A" — Would pay you $10,000/mo after taxes if you were well and working and $0/mo if you were sick or hurt and unable to work.

OR

Job "B" —Would pay you $9,840/mo after taxes if you were well and working and $5000/mo after taxes if you were sick or hurt and unable to work.

The question is, "Which job would you take?"

If you chose Job "A", go to www.disabilitycanhappen.org and read up. If you chose Job "B" you decided to forego $160.00/mo of salary to buy yourself a comprehensive disability plan to protect you and your family in case something serious happens to you.

Sample annual premiums for a comprehensive individual disability plan are as follows (see Chart #2, below). Your rates may be 20% higher or lower depending upon how physically strenuous your work requirements are. These are costs per $1000/mo benefits, benefits payable to age 67.

Chart #2

Age	Male	Female
30	$370	$600
40	$600	$850
50	$700	$1,120

Discount these rates by 40% for the cost of a basic starter policy previously mentioned that can be upgraded over the next three to five years.

Retirement Contribution Protection Plan (RCPP) — At the very least, you should insure 100% of your retirement plan contributions in the event you become sick or hurt and are unable to generate enough income to make them. In fact, one of the first items to go is savings when disability strikes. Benefits from this policy serve as a substitute for your contributions and can be made to age 65 or 70, at which time you may receive a tax-free lump sum distribution to help complete your retirement savings.

Business Overhead Expense Insurance (BOE) — This policy covers most business expenses, including employee salaries, when your business revenue cannot. Some policies even cover the cost of a key person you hire as a replacement until you can either return or sell the business. The cost of overhead expense coverage is 30% that of individual disability insurance. The premiums are deductible as a business expense. Be sure to get a quote for overhead insurance for business protection. BOE can also be used to cover business loans lasting up to 24 months.

Business Reducing Term Disability Insurance (BRTDI) — Don't use personal or business overhead disability insurance to cover business loans. Use the unique BRTDI plan instead. This is the least expensive way to insure loan obligations in excess of 24 months. If your bank insists on disability insurance as collateral for your loan, talk to a broker about this policy. It is a perfect fit in this situation. Benefits can be structured to cover up to a 10-year loan.

Buy-Sell Disability Insurance — Eight out of 10 buy-sell agreements are not even partially funded with disability insurance. Most owners and/or partners have term life insurance because it is perceived to be so cheap, but partners simply don't perceive the disability buy-sell policy as a good value. This is unfortunate and, again, I believe most insurance advisors take the wrong approach when designing these plans. Perhaps the best approach is to use the insurance or a partial funding solution as a supplement to the working partner's ability to buy out the disabled partners, rather than a 100% solution and a price tag that makes owners walk. In most cases, some insurance is better than no insurance and if owners would accept the insurance as part of the answer, they wouldn't leave their partners with all the risks. Buy-sell policies have very few moving parts. There usually is a one-year elimination period during which time the partner must be totally disabled from his or her occupation; then, the lump sum benefit is paid to the working partner to provide the funds necessary to help buy out the disabled partner.

One-Way Buy-Out policies are also available. These are used when one partner wishes to buy out the other partner, but the reverse is not true.

Key-Man Disability Insurance — This policy will pay benefits to the company to provide the funds necessary to hire a replacement for a key person during his or her disability. If your company's future is tied very closely to the performance of one person, think seriously about mitigating the risk of losing them.

LONG-TERM CARE INSURANCE (LTCI)

LTCI is disability insurance for retirees. Instead of replacing lost income, like disability insurance, LTCI provides income to supplement retirement cash flow to help meet the additional costs of an extended long-term care event.

Long-term care is needed when you have a prolonged physical illness, disability or a cognitive impairment, such as Alzheimer's disease. Long-term care services may include help with daily living activities, home health care, assisted living, and nursing home care. The National Association of Insurance Commissioners (NAIC) published "A Shopper's Guide to Long-Term Care Insurance" that I strongly recommend you read. This guide discusses more about what long-term care services include, what Medicare and Medicaid will cover and what to look for when buying a long-term care insurance policy. The NAIC published this book in response to the clear message from Washington that the government doesn't think it can afford to cover these expenses, and that individuals should seriously consider private insurance. (The interactive tutorial located on my website, called "Understanding LTC" can help too.)

> A retirement cash flow projection will show whether or not you are self-insured for this risk, or if you need insurance to supplement your cash flow.

As comprehensive as this educational tool is, it was not designed to give you all the details you need to help you select the perfect LTCI policy. Therefore, I will explain what I believe is important when designing a policy.

First you must determine if you need LTC insurance. You many need the help of a financial advisor who can run your retirement cash flow projections, illustrating the impact a long-term care event lasting five years or more will have on those projections. This will show whether or not you are self-insured for this risk, or if you need insurance to supplement your cash flow.

Assuming you have a need, you then should find an insurance advisor who has been a LTCI specialist for at least five years. Ask for quotes from at least three different companies and a spreadsheet showing the significant pros and cons of each. A policy checklist is located in the back of the NAIC Shoppers Guide. A LTCI specialist should be able to go through this checklist with you to make sure you are not missing anything important.

Before you apply for coverage, make sure your agent has reviewed your health history to avoid being declined or receiving a higher premium than originally quoted. Underwriting criteria varies from company to company, so it may be possible to receive a better offer from one company than you would from another. A good agent will take this into account before applying for coverage. This pre-underwriting step is very important.

Sample annual premiums for a comprehensive individual Long-Term Care policy are as follows (see Chart #3, below). Costs are per $1000/mo of benefit. Benefits payable for life.

Chart #3

Male/Female		
Age	Lifetime Pay Premium Option	10 Pay Premium Option
45	$580.00	$1,670.00
50	$650.00	$1,620.00
55	$770.00	$1,850.00
60	$980.00	$1,920.00

Discount these rates by 25% to get the cost of policy with a five-year benefit period.

Here are some suggestions I have for policy design.

1. Choose a 90-day Elimination Period (E.P.). This can be less expensive than a 30- or 60-day E.P. and you are not likely to go bankrupt waiting a few extra months for benefits.

2. You can purchase riders (built–in with some policies) that reduce the E.P. to zero days if your care starts in your home. Each day you receive care in your home counts toward satisfying the waiting period for assisted living and nursing home.

3. Don't choose a benefit period of less than five years. I know statistics say the average nursing home benefit is less than that, but those statistics don't include home care or assisted living care. When those are added, the average is closer to five years. Statistically, women need care longer than men.

4. Purchasing a shared care rider adds flexibility to your and your partner's (spouse or domestic partner) policy. Instead of each of you purchasing a five-year policy, you jointly purchase 10 years of coverage. So if you need care for two years, your partner would have eight years of coverage remaining. In most cases, the unused portion of the deceased partner's coverage rolls over to the surviving partner free of charge. If you didn't buy a shared coverage rider, and using the same scenario above, your three years of unused benefits would be forfeited and would be unavailable to your partner for use.

5. Survivorship Waiver of Premium Rider (built-in to some policies) can also be a valuable feature. In general, this rider states that if a couple buys policies together and don't make a claim for at least 10 years (fewer years with some policies) and one of the partners dies, the surviving partner's premium is paid up for life. This rider is most attractive the further apart the life expectancies are of the couple.

6. Benefit Inflation Adjustments are essential, especially if you are under age 75. This rider will automatically increase your benefits by 5% each year to help preserve them against the erosive effects of inflation. A compounded inflation adjuster is recommended for those under age 65. A compound or simple adjuster can be used thereafter. A compound adjuster costs 20% more than a simple adjuster because a compound adjuster increases the policy benefit at a faster rate. For example, a compound adjuster will double your policy benefits every 15 years. A simple adjuster will double your policy in 20 years, but won't double them again for another 40 years. So, the longer away you are from a care event, the more valuable the compound inflation rider is. There is a third kind of inflation option that is not automatic, but voluntary. Every three years or so the insurer sends a letter to you asking if you would like to increase your benefits. If you say yes, your benefits are increased and your premium is increased accordingly. Be careful, if you say no for two consecutive options, you may lose your right to those increases again unless you go through medical underwriting, which may be difficult to do when you are in your 70's and 80's.

I hope the time you spent reading this chapter was worthwhile. Insurance planning can be difficult. I would like to re-emphasize the importance of hiring an independent financial advisor who can, for a fee, create a comprehensive financial plan for you. It all starts with a plan. The insurance is simply a means to support those plans.

John E. Ryan, CFP®
Ryan Insurance Strategy Consultants
5690 DTC Boulevard Suite 130-W
Greenwood Village, CO 80111
Tel: 800.796.0909
Fax: 888.337.2291
Email: john@ryan-insurance.net
www.ryan-insurance.net

ABOUT THE AUTHOR: John E. Ryan, an independent insurance broker since 1978, also is a CERTIFIED FINANCIAL PLANNER™, Financial Planning Association (FPA) member, and the owner of the Colorado-based insurance firm of Ryan Insurance Strategy Consultants. John focuses primarily on life, disability, and long-term care insurance planning for highly compensated professionals and executives. He consults with financial advisors, attorneys, CPAs, and their clients in addition to managing his own private insurance practice in Colorado.

John holds a Bachelor of Arts Degree in Economics from the College of the Holy Cross in Worcester, Massachusetts, and has conducted extensive insurance training classes through the Life and Disability Insurance Training Councils at the University of Notre Dame, University of New Hampshire, and the University of New Orleans.

His insurance expertise has led to a variety of speaking and teaching engagements throughout the country. He also has authored and participated in numerous industry-related articles for professional publications such as *Kiplinger's, Forbes, Broker World, NAPFA Advisor, Investment Advisor, The Physicians Personal Advisory, Northwest Physicians Magazine, Financial Planning* magazine, *Money* magazine, *Modern Maturity, Medical Economics, The Washington Post, AARP* magazine, *Time* magazine, *AICPA Journal,* National Public Radio (NPR), and CNBC.

John's lecture series includes: Recent Developments in the Disability Insurance Marketplace; Long-Term Care Insurance – Disability Insurance for Retirees; Life Insurance in the Estate Planning Process; Long-Term Care Insurance Plan Design Considerations; Choosing the Right Life, Disability, or Long-Term Care Insurance Policy for Your Clients; The Ten Most Common Mistakes in Life, Disability, Long-Term Care Insurance Planning; and How to Evaluate an Existing Cash Value Life Insurance Policy.

5. If We're So Successful, How Come We're Not Making Money?

Susan Winer
Stratenomics, Inc.

I t's the ancient, plaintive cry of every entrepreneur. You've read every book. You've sought the advice and counsel of everyone you know. You have a business plan and you are pretty sure you've followed it faithfully. So, after all that hard work — the sweat equity everyone talks about — what happened?

There's no easy answer to that question. Virtually everyone who starts a business shares the same objectives: to be successful, to have recognition, to have credibility, to have independence and freedom … and to make money. It's true; a company that is healthy, growing and successful will meet your personal and professional objectives (the reasons you started the company in the first place), and will be more than a "replacement paycheck"… way more. If your company continues to grow and revenues continue to increase it can support you and your family comfortably in the style to which you've become accustomed (or would like to become accustomed). You will have the financial resources to continue to successfully compete in the market, whether or not you remain at the helm. In other words, a healthy, stable, growing company builds shareholder value over the long term.

However, in too many cases something happens and the business and the business owner are faced with unanticipated problems for which there has been no preparation. This can happen no matter the size of the company or its revenues. Larger companies face the same problems as smaller ones. Companies that are 10 or 15 years old face many of the same barriers to continued success as organizations with only a few years of history.

Factors that Inhibit Growth and Defeat Success

1. Lack of planning: Very few businesses are under-capitalized; rather they are under-planned. It's the *use* of the capital that is often the issue. Growth is a *planned activity*, it doesn't just happen. It can, and should, be anticipated and managed. *Knowing what to do with available capital is as important as knowing how much you really need.*

2. Unrealistic ambitions or getting caught up in other people's perception of success. Success is not necessarily measured by size. Size and profitability are not always synonymous. Your business can be very big and very unprofitable or your business can be very small and very profitable. Knowing your capacity — what you can handle and what you want your company to look and feel like — and then growing your company (planning) based on those objectives is critical to its success. Trying to be what someone else wants you to be is a surefire way of running into trouble in business, and in life.

3: *The Ostrich Syndrome.* Ostriches are noted for sticking their head in the sand at the first sight of danger. For some reason, they actually think they are invisible and, therefore, invincible. The same concept holds true for the entrepreneur who avoids the signals that his or her company may be in trouble. Avoiding sitting down and figuring out what's really happening is akin to the line from "Alice in Wonderland" when the Queen of Hearts is asked by Alice what she is doing and she answers: "Now, here, you see, it takes all the running you can do, to keep in the same place." So, instead of sticking your head in the sand, ask yourself the following questions:

- Do I need a capital injection in order to respond to business opportunities, diversify, or maintain a competitive edge?

- Am I in the right marketplace now compared to where I was three or five years ago? Are there *new* markets for my products or services?

- Are there new services and products I can offer that are compatible with what I'm currently doing? Are there ways in which I can capitalize on existing technology and resources in my company without substantively altering my business model?

- Are my personal needs (financial, emotional and psychological) the same now as when I started my company? The same as three years ago? Last year? Do I still get excited about going to the office when I get up, and feel the same challenge and enthusiasm about what I'm doing?

- Have I lost control of my business? Has my business taken control of me?

4. Lack of delegation. Letting go of the need to micro-manage is an important part of growing a business. Building the appropriate infrastructure for your company gives you the ability to not have to worry about every single detail. It allows you to input new, fresh ideas from a different perspective, add the dimension that your company needs to flourish and sustain itself, and even permits you to take a vacation or a day off.

5. Maintaining an ego-centered company. (This is an elaboration of number four.) Many entrepreneurs think their companies cannot survive without them. The founder/owner feels the necessity to think of everything, and tries to do everything, often disempowering employees or standing in the way of progress, new ideas and new opportunities. When this happens, the intrinsic value of the company ends up being directly tied to the owner, the company and the person are so intertwined that no one else can realistically represent or speak on behalf of the company. If the doors close, if there is a drop in business, it can be directly traced to the "heart" of the business — its owner/founder. This kind of scenario clearly plays out the concept of "the buck stops here." The problem is that if the owner/founder wants to retire or sell the business, all those years of hard work may end up having little value in the market without the key person actively involved. It's hard to tell a customer who has always worked directly with the owner that the owner isn't going to be around any more.

In the eyes of the state, a company is a human being — an entity that has a life, a tax status, an identity. Just like a child, in order for a company to reach its full potential it must be allowed to grow up. At some point you have to cut the proverbial umbilical cord and give your "child" room to breath, to spread its wings. Like all of us, your business needs outside stimulation and needs to experience the energy, ideas and enthusiasm of others so that it isn't one-dimensional. Having an organizational model that incorporates other decision makers and other opinions and talents will contribute to creating a more robust business environment and a healthier company with greater value when it's time to sell or retire.

Building a Healthy Company

What constitutes a healthy company? Turn that question around a bit: how do you know if YOU are healthy ... if you have any hidden illnesses or diseases you should take care of before they get worse? Just as each of us should periodically undergo a rigorous and complete physical exam to mitigate any physical problems real or brewing, a company needs to determine whether or not it has the capacity and stamina to survive and flourish in changing economic and market environments over the long term.

Just as *you* don't want to be caught unaware and unprepared should you have a serious or debilitating illness, you need to know if there are areas within your organization, your management team, your marketing, product and service fulfillment capabilities or your company's financial strategies that could weaken it, cause stress or inhibit continued growth and flexibility.

The best time to look for symptoms of serious illness is *before* your company is on "life support." Here are some of the more obvious signals of a distressed or stagnant company:

- Not taking money out of the company to pay yourself, or lowering your salary because of poor cash flow.

- Not being able to pay for all of the expenses incurred.

- Not being able to make the kinds of purchases needed to support company operations.

- Not hiring the staff you really want to hire because they want more compensation than you can afford at this time.

- The phones aren't ringing at your firm as much as they are at your competition.

- Continuously infusing personal or borrowed capital to support existing operations.

- Shareholders and/or board members are uninvolved, uncommitted and disinterested in the direction the company is headed.

- Increased turnover, particularly in key professional or managerial positions.

- A downward spiral in financial ratings, shareholder value, or credit ratings has been downgraded.

- Inventory turnover has slowed and product is not moving as quickly.

- Sales are flat for more than two quarters.

- Key accounts start disappearing or stop returning calls.

- The atmosphere within the company has changed and morale is low.

- There appears to be an increasing number of erratic, inconsistent and poorly articulated management decisions being made by staff and by management.

Just two or three combined signals can weaken the body of a company and make it susceptible to fatal illness or even death.

Diagnosing a Company's Specific Areas of Weakness

Whatever the size of the company, the number of employees, the industry sector or revenues, the same **dynamics** for success and sustainability are at play.

Dynamic (according to the Merriam-Webster Dictionary) is defined as "an underlying cause of change or growth."

At the most basic level, a company's health is measured by looking at seven organizational Dynamics[1]:

- Leadership (Ability to perpetuate a culture of success)

- Decision-Making (Context for action)

- Marketability (Capacity to compete)

- Infrastructure (People, facilities, processes and technology)

- Communication (Clarity of message)

---

1 Dynamics and Critical Factor Discussion is adapted from The Corporate Fitness Report®, a proprietary product of Stratenomics, Inc.

- Execution (Ability to get the work done successfully)

- Adaptability (Facility to alter course)

Within each Dynamic there are various critical factors that, in aggregate, define the Dynamic, but individually show you where there are problems or weak links in the organization. For example, take **Leadership**. If you want to evaluate the ability within your company to perpetuate a culture of success, you would look at six critical factors:

- Is there is clarity of direction for employees and are they aware of direction given?

- Is there a commitment to success?

- Is there management team cohesiveness?

- Is there a commitment to employees, their well-being and stability within the company?

- How is the ability to manage (in general, and at all levels) defined and expressed?

- Do employees feel empowered?

Let's look at another Dynamic: **Marketability.** The critical factors you want to look at are:

- The relevance of your marketing plan to your strategic plan

- Awareness within your organization of market changes

- Relevance of pricing policies to marketing and company strategies

- Whether there is clarity and continuity in how you approach positioning the company compared to its competition

Adaptability is one of those corporate Dynamics that is often thought to be hard to measure and somewhat intangible. In fact, if you want to know whether your company can easily alter its course should there be changes in market conditions, the competitive environment or an economic downturn, then you would look at:

- The degree to which risk management and/or analysis is integrated into business operations

- The company's financial strength and how flexible the financial strategies

- Whether the organizational mindset is static or dynamic

- How easily and quickly decisions are made and acted upon

- How well management directs change

- If the company has the infrastructure and plan in place to support changes, if need be, for either growth challenges or survival

A company's **Infrastructure** defines its ability to support future business activity. In looking at this aspect of the business, you need to look at:

- How human resources are managed

- The kinds of quality control systems and standards in place

- Whether there are sufficiently robust systems for information and financial management

- Whether processes for handling customers and product/service fulfillment are in place and followed

- Sales history, activity and depth

Communication is critically important. Not just how you communicate to customers, prospects or other parties external, but how you communicate, and *what* you are communicating, internally. For example you should look at:

- How and whether internal conflicts are handled

- If there is room for discussion within and among management, employees, departments and/or business units

- How effective internal and external communications are

- What the process for information flow is within the company and to the public

A company can have the best plans, the best ideas and even the best products or services in the market, but this has no bearing on success if there is not the ability to do the work effectively and deliver the products or services. **Execution** is the by-word here and when you look at execution in your company you need to think about:

- Whether the company's strategic plan is actually being followed and institutionalized within the organization

- Whether there are policies in place for personnel, for handling all sales related activities, for managing the operations within a company

- Are these policies readily available to personnel and are they followed and reviewed regularly

- Is there resource depth in terms of the number of qualified personnel and technical capacity to support current and future business activity

- Are the skills and knowledge of employees being used effectively

- Do employees understand their responsibilities and respond effectively to what needs to be done?

Finally, what about **Decision-Making?** How are decisions made within the company, or, more to the point, *are they being made?* Among the ways to evaluate this for your company is to look at:

- Whether outside advisors and skilled experts are utilized

- How quickly are organizational or operational dysfunctions recognized and addressed

- Is there a formal strategic planning process and who is involved

- Is the process of decision-making perceived by employees and management as effective and consistent

The End of the Sentence

What happens if you've done everything right, or, at least, you are pretty sure you've done the right thing to protect the years and dollars you've invested in your business? What happens when it's time to think about retiring, selling the company, merging with another company, or, perhaps, just passing it on to the next generation? It's never too early in the corporate life cycle to think about these things. Most entrepreneurs act as if they will live — and work — forever. The measure of success for a company and an executive is to prepare for the future and to anticipate the unexpected.

Here are 10 common mistakes entrepreneurs make that can seriously affect the long-term value of their company and disrupt business operations. They are easy to avoid, but only if you know what to look for.

Checking Your Company's Pulse
(An Informal Assessment)

Here is a checklist of some of the key Critical Factors that influence or affect your company's internal health...how does your company score? On a scale of 1-5 (with 5 reflecting the highest score) rate your company?

THE FACTORS	RATINGS (circle number)
	weak ... strong
1. Clarity of direction	1 2 3 4 5
2. Management team cohesiveness	1 2 3 4 5
3. Consistency within organizational decision-making	1 2 3 4 5
4. Effectiveness of the decision-making processes	1 2 3 4 5
5. Clarity and continuity of product positioning	1 2 3 4 5
6. Relevance and applicability of:	
A. The management information system	1 2 3 4 5
B. Quality control systems and standards	1 2 3 4 5
C. Technology utilization	1 2 3 4 5
7. Human resources ability to fulfill critical functional needs	1 2 3 4 5
8. Management's ability to direct change	1 2 3 4 5
9. Influence and motivation of the owners and/or investors	1 2 3 4 5
10. Corporate responsibility to:	
A. Employees and shareholders	1 2 3 4 5
B. The community and customer-base	1 2 3 4 5

An average score of three or below is a clear warning sign of serious problems internally and you should consider taking immediate action to do a more in-depth diagnostic. If you have scored four or five consistently, you most likely have a healthy company and a strong potential for realizing the goals that you set when you started your business.

Number One: Failure to plan; aka, procrastination.

Number Two: Failure to obtain the proper valuation of your business.

Number Three: Failure to take the time to identify who would succeed you in the event you decide to sail around the world without your computer or blackberry, or intend to retire, or have the opportunity to sell the business.

Number Four: Failure to integrate your business succession plan into your estate plan.

Number Five: Failure to plan for disability. What is your fall-back plan if you're injured and unable to work for four to eight months? Who would run the business? Make decisions?

Number Six: Failure to communicate your plans to key employees.

Number Seven: Failure to ensure that key assets remain with the business during any succession transfer. (Note: this is the case if you haven't communicated your plans to key employees and received their input.)

Number Eight: Failure to ensure that key personnel have access to the information needed to successfully run the business.

Number Nine: Failure to communicate desires, values, wishes and concerns to family and personnel.

Number Ten: Failure to have conflict resolution procedures in place before a dispute arises internally or with outside parties.

Some Closing Thoughts

As Donald Trump once said on his television program, *The Apprentice:*

*"In business, when things aren't working,
it's time to mix it up."*

The famous hotelier Conrad Hilton liked to tell his management team that:

*"Success seems to be connected with action.
Successful people keep moving.
They make mistakes, but they don't quit."*

Since the goal for every entrepreneur or for anyone starting or building a business is to be successful, then it stands to reason that taking the temperature of one's company periodically is a very good idea. It is important to see how the company is doing and determine whether any problems need to be addressed or corrected, and to keep your company on track for future growth and opportunity. Giving your company an annual "physical exam" is an excellent way to stay ahead of the competition and protect your investment. Not only do you get answers you need in order to make informed decisions and prepare for future opportunities, but your staff, shareholders, customers and/or clients will also benefit from this effort.

Susan Winer, President
Stratenomics, Inc.
1700 W. Irving Park Road
Chicago, IL 60613
Tel: 773.296.0015
Email: susan.winer@stratenomics.com
http://www.stratenomics.com

ABOUT THE AUTHOR: Susan Winer is President of Stratenomics, Inc., a Chicago-based firm that helps small and mid-cap privately held companies define and implement their strategic market, financial and organizational objectives. The firm's proprietary products are:

* The Corporate Fitness Report®
* The Corporate Living Will™

These products are widely respected resources for advisors and companies.

6. So ... You Want to Leave Your Business Someday?

Cynthia Turoski, CPA/PFS, CFP®
Bonadio Wealth Advisors

"Some day" will be here
before you know it!

C lose your eyes and imagine: You're doing everything you always wanted to do after exiting your business. You're on to your next adventure, possibly retired and spending new-found leisure time with family, grandchildren, and friends. You are doing more traveling, golfing, and finishing projects you never had the time to complete, and much more. Perhaps you've moved on to another business venture.

Now imagine this scenario: You are still involved with your business, but have fewer responsibilities and demands on your time. You're enjoying going to work every day, but you do so knowing you don't *have* to — it's by choice. You got what you needed from your business to secure your family finances and to carry you through a possibly long retirement. The ownership and management transition plan was well-structured — you feel confident the business will continue on as you had always envisioned. You don't worry about being able to collect on buyout payments; the business is sound even without your day-to-day oversight. Or maybe you sold to an outside third party and walked away with the highest possible value and best possible payment terms.

Sounds wonderful, doesn't it? But, wait a minute — rewind. How can all of this happen? How did you get to this point? Did all of these pieces fall into place by chance all by themselves?

Ah … no. Of course not. It took thoughtful pre-planning.

But before we discuss exit strategies, let me tell you about a situation that my colleague and succession planning team leader, Gordon Robbie, was involved in recently. The founder of a contracting company came in to meet with Gordon about his business exit planning needs. The founder is in his 60's and started the company more than 30 years ago. In our geographic area, the company is recognized as the leader in its field.

He brought his three sons into the business with him – all now having equal ownership with their father. The boys' strengths complement each other well: One son is more sales-oriented, another is good in field operations; the other son is finance-oriented and handles the general management of the company.

The father divorced a few years ago. There was no buy/sell agreement in place. Luckily, he reached an out-of-court settlement with his wife without having to give her part of the business. Now, two of his sons are going through a divorce. One divorce may easily be settled, but the other is highly contested. The value of the business comprises the majority of the latter son's personal net worth. He doesn't have much else to balance out the marital asset division without using the value of his company stock. There still is no buy/sell agreement in place to address how the stock would be handled in a divorce situation. The stock is dangling out there – at risk of passing into the wrong hands. Possibly, the other family members could find themselves in business with the divorced wife.

Another problem recently surfaced that is causing conflict among the sons. One son has been running his personal expenses through the business. His wife has run up a sizable company credit card balance. The son who is the general manager discovered this and wants it resolved immediately. We have seen situations like this where issues and conflicts progress to the point where family ties disintegrate and they no longer can get along or agree on business decisions.

There is no telling the outcome at this point. Possible perils include:

- The company stock falling into the hands of someone they don't want to be partners with — the ex-wife — and the conflicts this could create.

- An excessive allocation of personal assets to the wife in the divorce settlement to keep her away from the company stock.

- A lack of harmony and trust among the brothers as a result of the one brother's wrongdoing.

Once the divorces are settled, the father and his sons need to focus on putting a buy/sell agreement in place that mandates what happens with the company stock under these circumstances. The best time, of course, to put a buy/sell agreement in place is when everyone gets along and is cooperative — before there are issues and conflicts. In this case, they need to resolve this task before it becomes more difficult to come to agreement on the terms — harmony has already skipped a beat.

These aren't the only issues. For example, who would run the company when the father transitions out or dies? The father's estate plan provides for his stock to pass equally to his three sons, leaving them as equal remaining owners. There is no heir apparent to company leadership, if it even should be one of the sons. The leader should be selected based on competency, not entitlement. Someone has to be the leader to take the reins of running the company. The father did not want to be put in the uncomfortable situation of making that choice. But if he doesn't make a decision, the company could flounder, with the sons possibly pulling in different directions, jeopardizing their relationship along the way.

It's pretty reasonable to see that this is not where the father wants things to be. Without intervention and proactive measures, he won't get the end result he is looking for. It doesn't happen by chance.

What is Exit Planning?

Let's back up. What is the definition of "Exit Planning" and what does it really mean to you?

Exit planning is a systematic process that provides the business owner with a comprehensive and strategic approach to the orderly transition of the management and ownership of his/her company on his/her own terms and schedule. Contingencies are built into the plan to provide for the chance that the owner dies or becomes disabled prior to the planned exit.

The process should involve the following steps:

1. Establish owner objectives and vision for the future of the business
2. Determine value/price
3. Selection and concurrence
4. Maximize, preserve, protect company value
5. Transfer of ownership
6. Continuity planning
7. Communicate
8. Personal wealth management

Although exit planning and succession planning are terms commonly interchanged, we will use the term exit planning in this chapter. An exit plan may involve a wind-down and liquidation of the company. Otherwise, it could involve a transfer of the business to another person by sale or gift to a family member. It could also involve a sale to another insider such as a key person or other co-owners, or it could involve a sale to an outside party.

A well-thought-out exit plan can provide numerous benefits for the company. Benefits such as continuity and legacy of the business, retention of key employees, minimization of the tax burden, and preservation of company value, are just a few of the key advantages. The business owner can retire in comfort, provide for family, and breathe a sigh of relief knowing they have their full estate plan in order.

Most business owners, and some advisors, think of exit planning as simply having a buy/sell agreement and a life insurance policy. That's not the end of the story. Even a single owner needs an exit plan, but may not need a buy/sell agreement. Life insurance funding may be important, but that is only used for transfers at death. What about transfers during lifetime? Others hire top-notch estate planning specialists to design an estate plan using family limited liability companies and trusts, thinking the estate plan accomplishes their exit planning. They fail to take a more holistic view. Estate planning techniques are just a tool used in exit planning.

The terms on the next page are some of the possible TECHNIQUES you can use when transferring the business. However, no one knows what the best strategy is for you without knowing the rest of the exit planning pieces.

Business Transfer Planning Techniques	
• Installment sale	• Stock bonus plan
• Sale to an Intentionally Defective Grantor Trust	• Phantom stock plan
	• Annual exclusion gifting
• Self-canceling installment note	• Bequest
• Gift to a dynasty trust	• Charitable remainder trust
• Grantor retained annuity trusts (GRATs)	• Employee stock ownership plan
• Outright gift	• Sale-leaseback
• Voting and nonvoting stock recapitalization	• Cross-purchase
• Transfer of the business to a family limited liability company	• Stock redemption
	• Preferred stock recapitalization

Less than 30% of private businesses have an achievable succession plan in place. Most business owners do nothing — as they say, failing to plan is the same as planning to fail — or they choose to focus on one element of the exit planning process and neglect other equally important issues, often leading to a poor outcome for the business and all involved.

The sidebar on page 84, Exit Planning: A Complete Process, illustrates the perils of failing to engage in the *full* exit planning process.

The exit planning process should include a customized, holistic, multidisciplinary approach to designing and implementing your successful exit from your business. The exit planning process helps you assess your options based on the time frame available as well as the tax situation and financial position of the business and the individuals involved, with the objective of fulfilling your personal goals. The process helps maximize the financial return, minimize tax liability, plan for contingencies and increase the likelihood of a successful transfer of the business.

The Importance of Exit Planning

As a business owner, you take many risks, but not planning for this event could be one of your greatest risks of all. It is very likely the biggest business and financial event of your life. Not only does it affect your employees' lives, but your and your family's entire financial future may also depend on it. If you're like most business owners, the value of the business comprises most of

Exit Planning: A Complete Process

Let us tell you about the owners of SOS Construction ...

John and Don were the owners of this highly profitable construction company. They wanted to get out of the business and wanted to know how to do so. As successful as they were, they were tired of the government regulations, changing tax codes and day-to-day grind of running a multi-million dollar company.

They couldn't sell to a third party because neither was willing to stay on after a sale – and they had failed to develop a strong management team, which any savvy purchaser would require as a condition of purchasing the company. Transferring ownership to a group of key employees was also out of the question. None had been groomed to take on this type of responsibility and nothing had been done to fund this type of buyout. Both owners were too young to have business-active children.

Their only option was to liquidate.

John and Don's highly profitable company had little worth beyond the value of its tangible assets. After the sale of those assets, dozens of employees lost jobs, the business disappeared, and John and Don left millions of dollars on the table.

You can see from this example that John and Don's buy/sell agreement and life insurance funding didn't even come into play to solve their situation. Real exit planning involves much more – it is much more complex and comprehensive. Had they engaged in full exit planning, perhaps John and Don would have had more available options resulting in more cash in their pockets while the successful business they created could carry on under different ownership. ◆

your personal net worth. Many business owners plan to sell the business and retire, often expecting for that to be the bulk of their retirement funding. That sounds well and good, however they typically have not taken the steps necessary to make that vision a reality. Despite having built successful, profitable companies, many are not successful in getting the optimal value for the company on the sale to an outsider or in completing the transition of ownership and management to the next generation. The survival rate of family businesses into subsequent generations is dismal. It is a commonly known fact that 30% of family businesses make it to the second generation of family ownership and management and 15% make it to the third generation. That is rather astounding when you stop to consider that about 90% of all U.S. businesses are family owned or controlled. The primary cause for failure? Lack of planning.

Take note, you *will* leave your business eventually — voluntarily or otherwise. You're not alone in this challenge. At any given time, 40% of business owners are facing the issue of ownership transfer or sale. Most don't face it head-on, thoroughly or early enough. That could result in forced liquidation rather than the better scenario of transferring it to an insider, such as a family member involved in the business, a key employee or a co-owner, or selling to an outside party.

Failure to plan is typically because:

- You have simply been too busy working *in* the business with no time to work *on* the business.

- You may be unsure of how to begin planning for your exit, who to rely on for help, or even where to begin, so you delay and put if off.

- You're not anxious to have to choose one child over another to lead the business or aren't confident enough in his or her qualifications to take over the business.

- The cost of proper planning has been an obstacle; and/or

- You're hesitant to think that far ahead because you're not sure what you would do with your time or how you might feel when you are no longer in control.

Lack of planning could be costly — more so than the cost of devising a strategy. Lack of planning could also lead to cash flow problems for the business should an improperly structured transition event occur. One of the biggest reasons businesses fail is because they run out of money. Maximizing and managing business cash flow is vital to the business's health and sustainability. Insufficient cash flow (perhaps from having to buy out an owner from current cash flow or to cover income or estate taxes or even from management ill-prepared to take on new, bigger responsibilities) can dry up a company, leaving the company unable to operate, pay back loans, or keep employees and customers — causing a downward spiral of the business. Planning is crucial.

Reasons You May Want to Exit Your Business

Most owners think only of death or retirement as events they need to provide for, however there are a number of other reasons why you may want or need to exit your business. To name just a few:

- Boredom
- Desire to change lifestyle
- Owner burnout or complacency
- Health problems or disability
- Family or spousal pressure
- Divorce
- An offer to sell you cannot refuse
- Competition
- No need to "prove" anything to anyone anymore
- Unwilling to commit to new requirements for new level of debt or equity to take the company to the next level
- Changing economic, political, tax or business conditions
- Decreasing tolerance for risk
- Loss of product or service viability
- Loss of franchise, distributorship, lease, major customer or supplier, key employee, or patent
- Unable or unwilling to keep up or catch up with technology advancements

Any of these can speed up your timeline by changing your situation and leading to a desire or need to exit your business much sooner than expected. These are not typically reasons that can be foreseen and planned for like a "scheduled" retirement transition could be. Some of these triggers — like competition, changing environment, or loss of product or service viability — could lead to your business becoming worthless except for the underlying assets it owns. Liquidation may then be your only exit option. Your personal financial security could be at risk if, indeed, you haven't diversified your personal net worth and were counting on a higher value for retirement. Other triggers prove the need to get the process started as early as possible.

The Exit Planning Process

So where do you even begin? First, seek professional guidance. Even if you had spare time to devote to this process (highly unlikely!), too many issues come into play to go it alone — successfully. You need to find a professional who specializes in exit planning and who can oversee and coordinate the entire process. This professional will know which other specialists to bring in, and when, in order to complete your advisory exit planning team. This team approach can help you resolve the business, financial, legal, tax, family and emotional issues that come into play.

Step 1: Determining Owner Objectives and Vision for the Future of the Business

This step helps you create your "wish list" of what you want and the minimum parameters required to meet your needs. Establishing your personal objectives is vital to being able to even proceed through the process with any meaning and direction. How can any solutions be devised without knowing what you want or need from the process? You and any other owners also need to develop goals for the business. What is your vision for the business? If you don't know where you are going, how will you be able to get there? You'll be flying blind.

Your exit planning team should help you determine:

- How long you wish to work in the business and in what capacity — you may wish to stay involved in the business, but not in the same role

- What your vision is for the future of the business

- Who you want to transfer the business to, if anyone:
  - ► Family
  - ► Co-Owner
  - ► Employee(s)
  - ► Outside third-party

- Who will lead the business and why should you choose that person

- How much you want or need from the business to meet your personal financial needs

  This helps determine if you can afford to gift your ownership to family members should you so desire, or must you sell it, and in what timeframe and at what pace do you need the income stream.

  CPA financial planners can perform this analysis since they have a unique understanding of the business and personal finance and tax issues based on the entity's legal structure.

- If it is important to you to:

  ▸ Get full value for the business

  ▸ Transfer wealth to children. If so, when, in what form (cash, ownership) and in what amounts

  ▸ Provide a benefit to key employees at the time of sale — in cash or ownership

Identifying your goals is an important first step, but how can you reach those goals if you don't set a course to achieve them? You have a better chance of making your goals a reality if you plan early enough. This process takes time. The earlier you start, the more options you'll have.

Your exit planning team should help you manage the goals and expectations of the family in keeping with what is truly feasible to fulfill your objectives, always with the continuity of the business in the forefront of their minds. The team should work with you to seek competent people to run the company and continue its success. Your team can help you manage situations where family members feel entitled to company ownership or to provide in other ways for family members who aren't involved in the business.

To provide information to determine how to proceed further, you must know the value of the business in order to assess what options are available to meet your established goals.

Step 2: Determining Value/Price

The business is usually the owner's most valuable asset. A typical owner objective is to turn the business wealth into a liquid resource to support the owner's desired lifestyle in retirement. An estimated valuation of the company must be done in order to quantify its worth. In performing this valuation, it helps the valuation expert to know who you wish to transfer the business to from Step 1. The valuation expert can then determine the approach to be taken in valuing the business. You may need the highest possible value or the lowest defensible value, depending on to whom and how you will make the transfer. If you wish to sell to an outsider, you would want the highest possible value. If you wish to gift some or all of the business to a child working in the business, you would want the lowest defensible value.

Step 2 determines what you have — how much the business is worth and how much cash flow the business can generate for exit planning. The current value and projected cash flow are determining factors in evaluating the direction and planning tools available to reach your objectives. Knowing the approximate value of the business helps determine what you could get for your business so you can determine when you can afford to leave your business. A valuation expert is, therefore, integral to the exit planning team.

The valuation:

- Helps determine the marketability of the business should you wish to sell now

- Provides insight into what factors are pertinent in driving the value of the business in order to enhance it or deflate it

- Allows advisors to evaluate the tax consequences of various exit strategies

- Allows advisors to estimate the cash flow effect to the buyer and the seller to determine if your objectives can be met now or if there must be more preparation

If the value is insufficient to meet your personal financial needs, then you should focus on improving the value.

Step 3: Selection and Concurrence

From Step 1, you may have identified who you think would be a good successor. However, your team will be able to help you objectively select a candidate who is truly qualified based on pertinent criteria, not entitlement. The most qualified candidate may very well be unrelated to the family.

Once you have properly identified your successor and have an understanding of the business's value, you can't proceed further without asking if that candidate is even interested in taking on management and/or ownership of the business. You need to learn about his/her personal goals and expectations. You need to find out what personal financial resources he/she has with which to buy the company or his/her willingness to take on that obligation. It would be a waste of time and money to skip that step. Even the best plan can fall apart when incorrect assumptions are made and the wrong direction is taken.

Step 4: Maximizing and Protecting Business Value

Value drivers maximize the value of the business and protect the value you have worked so hard to build. These value drivers help make the business healthier long-term, no matter who you wish to transfer the business to.

In this step, your team helps you identify which value drivers are important to meeting your overall exit objectives and devise specific steps to maximize the impact of the value drivers. Some ways to improve the value of the business include:

- Increase cash flow
- Develop operating systems that improve the sustainability of cash flows
- Improve the facility's appearance
- Pay down debt
- Document the sustainability of earnings
- Implement a strategy to grow the company
- Build a strong management team through training and development

Not all of these value drivers apply to everyone. Some only apply if you are intending to sell to an outsider. Others, like building a strong management team, apply no matter what your plans are for transferring the business.

The company's key employees are the company's most valuable asset. It is imperative to the company's continuing success (now and after transfer) to motivate them to excel and to remain with the company. Keeping and motivating key employees is the best way to:

- Increase the company's income stream and profitability
- Provide potential buyers for the business where others may not exist
- Increase business value by providing a capable management team for the new owner

If the company doesn't have all the key people it needs, an HR consultant can help recruit the right person(s).

One way to attract or reward key employees is to make sure the qualified retirement plans adequately provide for the higher-paid executives – within the law. A retirement plan consultant can determine if the current employer-sponsored plan can be improved upon. If contributions to highly compensated key employees are already maximized or if you want to benefit key employees even more, you could evaluate a key employee bonus plan.

Any key employee bonus plan should be formalized, tied to performance standards, be substantial so it motivates, and "handcuff" the key employee to the business. There are a number of strategies to reward key employees monetarily such as:

- Ownership equity plan, including:
  - ► Stock bonus
  - ► Stock option — nonqualified and incentive stock options
  - ► Stock purchase
- Cash-based plan, including:
  - ► Cash bonus
- Nonqualified deferred compensation plan
- Stock appreciation rights plan
- Phantom stock plan
- A combination of stock and cash

Taking care of key employees helps preserve and promote value. To *protect* value from taxing authorities, the team must consider the form of business entity (S vs. C Corporation, LLC, etc.) to plan for minimizing the tax impact of any transfer.

Step 5: Transferring Ownership

Based on the previous steps, you should have direction on how and to whom you will transfer ownership whether by sale to an insider or to an outside buyer.

Sale to an Outside Party

If you wish to sell the business to an outside party, your exit planning team would help you obtain the most beneficial sale price and terms. Most often, the business owner would want a cash sale of the business versus a drawn-out payment period when selling to an outsider. This avoids the risk of default.

Prior to sale, you must do some planning such as assessing with your exit planning team whether the sale should be an asset sale or a stock sale and pricing the business. Then you would market the business and find a buyer with the expert guidance from the exit planning team. The team would then help you negotiate the sale followed by documenting and closing the deal.

Keep in mind that with the aging of the population, it could become more and more difficult to find a qualified buyer willing to buy your company or pay the price you want — there may be a glut of sellers and fewer buyers. The stronger your company is, the better your chance of finding a buyer in that competitive environment.

Transferring Ownership to Insiders

If you have identified an insider to transition your business and leadership to, it is imperative that you groom the individual to take on such a role. Give them a little rope, let them see how you do things and what the thinking is behind your decisions, let them grow, gain confidence, gain experience.

When selling to an insider who you know and have groomed to be the successor, you may be more inclined to receive some portion of the sale price over time. This is especially true when transferring to family members. Insiders often have limited resources and cash with which to buy the business. Paying over time is often their only option. Your findings in **Step 1** help you better understand the minimum amount and the timeframe over which you can accept the payments in order to meet your personal financial needs.

When selling to an insider, you would likely have more options to stay involved in the business until you are satisfied that cash flow can be sustained.

Should you wish to gift the business to involved family members, a number of lifetime gifting strategies are possible — many that minimize the business value using discounts. No one technique fits everyone — the gifting strategy must be customized for your unique situation and in keeping with the nuances of the industry you are in.

Step 6: Continuity Planning for the Business

To plan for the contingency that you die or become disabled, you should plan now as if you are going to depart tomorrow.

Whether the company is a sole proprietor or has multiple owners, the same issues exist if you or another owner dies or becomes disabled before the planned exit, including:

- Continuity of business ownership
- Loss of financial resources

- Loss of key talent — the owner(s)

- Loss of employees and customers from the fall-out

If you are a sole proprietor, formalized communication of your wishes should designate which key employees should assume the responsibility to run the company. Your will can include a provision for passing the business to a family member who is involved in the business (you would need to consider any estate tax ramifications and make sure you provide financially for your spouse in other ways). Life insurance can help fund operations during the transition period. If there is a prospective purchaser of the business, such as a key person or an outsider, a buy/sell agreement with life and disability buy-out insurance funding should be put in place.

A multi-owner company should make sure they have a properly structured buy/sell agreement in place with adequate funding for life and disability buy-out options. This enables the other owners or the company to buy the owner's interest.

The buy/sell agreement should account for all the possible events that would trigger a stock transfer, such as:

- Death

- Disability — typically of 12-24 months or more

- Retirement

- Voluntary and involuntary termination of employment

- Involuntary transfer due to divorce or bankruptcy

- Transfer to a third party

- Business dispute among the owners

The terms of the stock purchase must be coordinated with the entity's legal structure and tax situation. The ownership and beneficiary designations on the insurance must be properly aligned with the terms of the stock purchase. So often we see the wrong ownership and beneficiaries on the insurance. The money could end up in the hands of an individual with no contractual obligation to buy the stock or cause unnecessary tax ramifications. Other times we see inadequate life insurance funding and no disability buy-out funding (disability buy-out insurance is different from income replacement disability insurance coverage).

In addition to a buy/sell agreement, there ideally should be a successor management plan in place.

Step 7: Communicate

Once the plan is formulated, your team will help you explain and discuss the plan with everyone who is affected by it. This fosters buy-in and commitment from the stakeholders while resolving conflicts.

Step 8: Personal Wealth Management

Once you have transferred the business and actual numbers are evident, you should revisit your personal wealth management needs. Specialists on your team can review your overall financial and estate plan, help you properly manage newly acquired liquid wealth, and coordinate any strategies from an income tax, estate/gift/trust, and financial perspective.

While you should revisit your estate plan after the transition, please don't wait until then to shore up your current estate plan. Something could happen to you "tomorrow." Your estate planning documents should be coordinated with your business, financial and tax situation. Trusts in your will need to be properly structured for the type of legal entity your business is, assets need to be properly titled, beneficiaries need to be carefully reviewed and aligned, liquidity needs to be planned for to provide for family and to pay estate administration expenses and taxes, etc. Please do it today. We see far too many holes in business owners' estate plans or many who do not even have an estate plan. According to a 2007 American Family Business Survey, nearly a third (31.4%) of business owners have no estate plan beyond a will.

Your Exit Planning Team

Some owners may try to do their own exit planning because they want to save on professional fees or think it is easier to do than it really is – they don't realize the complexities involved in doing it properly. *They don't know what they don't know.* An owner's successful transition from the business requires the coordination of many different elements. When all of these components have been considered and are working together, the end result is a successful transition from the business — on the owner's terms.

There are many business and personal issues to consider that require expertise from many different disciplines. No single individual possesses all the deep technical, consultative and relevant skills needed to develop the best possible exit plan. A coordinated team of exit planning specialists representing multiple disciplines should lead the way. They have the expertise to anticipate and identify potential problems that, otherwise, may go unrecognized.

A multidisciplinary approach to this process is a very powerful methodology for business owners to achieve and implement an integrated, comprehensive and widely accepted exit plan. This approach allows the business owner to draw on the experiences and expertise of several advisors who will work together as a team, to assist the business owners and the interested parties in defining and meeting their strategic goals.

Members of your team should have experience working together to constructively develop the integrated components of an exit plan. The team can't be effective for you if they can't work together for your benefit. The right team can manage the whole process for you by providing all the people, tools, and strategies necessary to achieve a successful business exit while preserving your interests in the process.

Members of your team may consist of:

- CPA business consultants, tax advisors, and valuation experts
- CPA financial planners
- Attorneys
- Insurance and investment advisors

Be careful when selecting your team members. Not every one of the above professionals will necessarily have experience specifically in exit planning or in working with closely-held businesses.

Let's face it — you have only one exit. You shouldn't trust it to someone untrained in the exit planning process.

Summary

Exit planning is a process, not an event. It takes time and professional guidance. The longer you wait to work through this process, the fewer choices you will have, the less likely you will be able to meet your goals, and the costlier the outcome from a financial and quality-of-life perspective for you, your family and your employees.

Remember, it takes time and significant effort to build a successful business. Isn't it worth devoting the time and effort necessary to plan a successful exit?

◆◆◆

Cynthia L. Turoski, CPA/PFS, CFP®
Managing Director/Owner
Bonadio Wealth Advisors of The Bonadio Group
6 Wembley Court
Albany, NY 12205-5808
Tel: 518.464.4080
Email: cturoski@bonadio.com

ABOUT THE AUTHOR: Cynthia Turoski has more than 20 years of tax and financial experience. She provides consultative services to a wide variety of clients, specializing on closely held business owners. Her unique background in personal and business tax and finance enables her to understand the business, financial and tax issues inherent with each form of business entity and their effect on the owner's personal finances. She has seen how imperative it is to have such a deep understanding of these issues in order to properly advise a business owner on his/her personal financial affairs.

Cindi has her AICPA designation as a Personal Financial Specialist, a CERTIFIED FINANCIAL PLANNER™ license, and B.S. in Accounting. Cindi focuses her advanced-level training on wealth management and transfer strategies.

Cindi frequently speaks and authors on financial planning and related topics and has been quoted in various news segments and publications, including *Practical Accountant, InvestmentNews, Journal of Financial Planning, Fortune Small Business, Albany-Colonie Chamber's Vision Magazine, New York's Tech Valley Relocation Handbook,* and *Saratoga* and *Glens Falls Business Journals.* Her article was featured on the front cover of *Construction Business Owner* magazine.

Gordon Robbie, CPA, Managing Partner
The Bonadio Group - Albany Office
Email: grobbie@bonadio.com

SPECIAL CONTRIBUTOR: Gordon's more than 35 years of experience as a CPA includes expertise with closely-held businesses, particularly in the construction industry. Gordon has extensive experience with, and an understanding of, the issues that closely held companies and their owners face and how they can develop and implement effective business solutions. In addition to providing traditional accounting services, Gordon is well known for providing consulting services, including business succession planning, operational reviews, retreat facilitation, mergers and acquisition, and retirement planning.

Gordon is a Partner in The Bonadio Group, a CPA and Business Advisory Firm headquartered in Rochester, New York. He is the Managing Partner of the firm's Albany Office, a member of the firm's Executive Committee, and Team Leader for the firm's Construction Group.

7. Business Transitions: What Do I Do After I Sell My Business?

Josh Patrick, CFP®
Stage 2 Planning Partners

M any private business owners' dreams come true the day they sell their businesses and convert their illiquid asset to a pile of cash. There are four ways business owners can exit their businesses, each providing a different way of receiving cash for the years of hard work and little pay. While immediate liquidity is not available for each of the four ways, all of them *do* provide psychological challenges that often dwarf the challenge of what to do with the cash.

The Four Ways to Leave Your Business

The four ways that an owner can leave his or her business and receive cash when they do so are:

1. **Selling the business to an outsider.** This option should always be an immediate liquidity event: the more upfront cash from the buyer, the better.

2. **Selling the business to an insider (managers).** When you sell to an insider, true liquidity is rarely achieved. Your money will often come to you in dribbles over several years. The one exception to this is if the selling owner decides to sell the company to an ESOP (Employee Stock

Ownership Program).

3. **Selling the business to family members.** Like selling the business to insiders, selling to family rarely results in a true immediate liquidity event. However, when properly structured, this option can provide more money to the seller than any of the other options.

4. **Liquidating the business.** This is always an immediate liquidity event. Unfortunately, in many cases, creditors take all of the cash with nothing left for the selling owner.

If your goal is to provide an immediate infusion of cash for personal use, a third-party sale (option one on page 97) will give you a higher probability of receiving cash upfront. At the same time, a third-party sale sometimes offers more psychological challenges than the other options (with the exception of a forced liquidation of your business, which usually carries the most stress).

The External Sale

The external sale represents a classic immediate liquidity event. The owner of the private business negotiates with an outside buyer who provides the selling owner with a significant cash windfall. After the sale closes, the selling owner has two questions to answer: How will the money be invested? How will time be spent now that he or she is no longer involved in running the business?

The goal of a third-party sale should always be to maximize the amount of money the selling owner receives. I strongly suggest that you engage a highly qualified intermediary (business broker, investment banker or middle market specialist) to help in the process. The type of intermediary you use depends on the size of the business you are selling.

If the sale price is less than $2 million, a business broker is likely to be the best choice. If the sale price is between $2 to $10 million, a middle market specialist is usually ideal. For sales totaling $10 million, the work of an investment banker is recommended. Once the sale reaches $50 million or more, engaging the services of the entire investment bank becomes necessary. These professionals are adept at helping the private business maximize the amount of money realized from a business sale. Any owner who engages in selling the business without professional help puts his or her potential financial rewards at risk.

The other issue that comes with selling a business to a third-party revolves around how to fill your time after the sale is made.

In many cases, a business owner is asked to stay on for a period of time in order for a smooth transition to take place. You may be asked to stay on and help for a short while after you sell your business. However, once the transition period is over, the new owner will want you out of the picture as quickly as possible. During the sales process you will hear about how important you are to the business, but that is a ploy to get you to sell your business for less money. The reality is that once the transition has been made, the new owners want to run the show without your interference.

After you leave your business you may feel like you have stepped off a cliff and fallen into an abyss. Your contacts stop calling, and those who used to ask for your advice no longer do so. Many selling owners have serious self-esteem issues that surface during the first 18 months following the sale of a business. Below are some considerations regarding the non-economic part of your potential sale:

- Have a realistic understanding of what the new business owners expect from you in terms of input.

- Know what the first six months of not controlling your company will look like. I suggest that you write yourself a memo on this topic.

- Spend a significant amount of time contemplating the next challenge.

- Have a clear understanding, from a financial planning point of view, as to where you are if you no longer collect a regular paycheck. (Usually, when a former business owner is fired, the employment contract is bought out in a lump sum.)

- If you think you will have a significant role in the company after the business is sold, make sure there is an intermediary who understands how to negotiate an employment contract. Such contracts often have a lower probability of a summary firing after the transition takes place.

- Have a local support system in place to help make the transition less difficult for you. It is often helpful to develop relationships with people who have gone through similar transitions in their lives.

Consider getting help from your financial advisor or wealth coach to work through the following issues if you are contemplating selling your business to an outside entity:

- Make sure your spouse or significant other is aware of what is likely to happen. Providing the family with tools, such as people to talk with, can help everyone successfully navigate the psychological side of selling the private business.

- Have something to do that will keep you engaged and make you feel valued after the sale of the business. Slowly begin to engage in other activities one to two years before selling the business. (This will also help increase the value of the business when it comes time to actually selling it.)

- Make sure there is an intermediary who understands sudden money events from both an economic and psychological point of view. This person should have extensive experience in finding appropriate team members to make the transition a positive one.

Often, Change is Hard

I sold my vending company in 1995. Before selling my company, I was one of the 10 best-known vending operators in the country. I received 10-15 phone calls a week from other vending operators and suppliers, asking my opinion on various issues facing our industry or our individual companies. I was in demand as a speaker, educator, and board member for various advisory bodies in our industry. However, the day I sold my company the calls stopped coming in. No one wanted my advice anymore. Although I had made a decision to move on and had started a new career, it was very lonely not having the phone ring and not having anyone ask for my advice.

After selling my vending machine company, I decided to enter a new field: life insurance. The loneliest two days I spent in my adult life were at my first sales meeting at a large mutual life insurance company. I was completely by myself. No one showed interest in meeting me or learning my story. It was difficult for me to transition from being a key person in an industry I knew to just another "new guy" in an industry I was just learning about.

These are rational and normal reactions for those who sell their businesses and start afresh. Some of these reactions occur because many selling owners do not know what will happen next. If they do know, they completely underestimate the effect it will have in their lives. The higher the profile you have in your industry, the tougher it will be for you to adjust to your new life after selling your business. ◆

Completing a sale to a third party usually takes about three years. As with all liquidity events, the line is not a straight one — along the way you might find that your center has been taken away from you. If this happens, it is important for you to gain a feeling of control over your life. It is challenging for you to make the transition from being in complete control to having other people control certain aspects of your life that have never been controlled by others before.

Selling to Managers

Most of the time, selling to your managers will not provide immediate liquidity. Business owners, in this scenario, usually do not receive a large chunk of cash at closing, but they do have the opportunity to gradually make the move away from active ownership.

> The challenge of making sure you put away enough money for the future is one of the biggest that you will have to deal with as a selling owner.

When selling owners hold papers for the sale of their businesses, they are likely to stay involved at some level to make sure the payments are made on a timely basis. It is often a good idea for selling owners to negotiate a reduced role in the business. This is a good way to gradually reduce time spent at the business while moving toward the new reality that comes with financial independence from the business, as well as reduced responsibility for the day-to-day operations of the old company.

Sellers of private businesses are used to getting paychecks. They often panic or, at the very least, feel uncomfortable living off of investments. The nature of the management buyout is often such that the owner continues receiving a paycheck — sometimes for a relatively long period of time. This can ease the selling owner into using investments as a source of income. For the first five years, the selling owner often receives some sort of salary continuation plan. This creates a better opportunity for the selling owner to understand how capital can be invested to produce the amount of cash needed on a monthly basis after the salary continuation plan ends.

The challenge of making sure you put away enough money for the future is one of the biggest that you will have to deal with as a selling owner. Often, there is a tendency for the seller to increase the level of his or her lifestyle during the first few years following the business sale. When you first sell your business, and receive a lump sum and, perhaps, a salary continuation, you might feel wealthy. Because much of the money from the sale of the business comes in the form of additional salary payments, the selling owner believes the money can all be spent immediately. When this mindset is prominent, it is no surprise when the seller runs out of money and is forced to find an activity that will provide the income necessary for the new lifestyle. Part of planning for the sale of your business is creating a budget that covers what can be spent now, and what must be saved from the business sale proceeds.

If you are contemplating an internal sale, make sure you have solid investments in place before beginning the process. You also need to clearly negotiate your future role in the business, how this role will change, and the expectations the buying owners have for you. Issues that should be addressed with an internal sale to managers include:

- A thorough financial and investment plan to make sure the sale will support financial independence for the seller of the business.

- Planning for the selling owner to move from active management to other engaging and fulfilling activities.

- A plan that allows the selling owner to maintain a significant role in the business while transitioning to a non-operating role.

- Encouraging the buying owners to welcome input from the selling owner for a period of time.

- Putting together a board of directors on which selling owners and buying owners can work in a cooperative manner.

The best part of an internal transaction is the non-financial part of the deal. The selling owner has an opportunity to gradually move from the role of active business owner to whatever comes next. This strategy is especially important when family is included; their needs and wants also should be integrated into the transition plan. If you are considering selling your business using an internal sale, you might find that a "discovery process" can allow you to find a new passion to pursue. This, combined with the internal nature of your sale, allows you the maximum probability of gradually removing yourself from day-to-day operations in a way that is smooth and emotionally satisfying.

Family Transitions

Rarely does transferring a business to family members provide a true liquidity event for the selling owner. In many respects, a family transition is economically similar to transferring your business to your management team. The obvious difference is that the family business transfer involves family issues as well as business issues. If you are contemplating selling your business to family members, it is important to understand the following issues: economic and financial independence issues, family dynamics, corporate governance and how many mouths the business can feed. Although there are more challenges to a family business transition than any other transfer method, the non-economic issues often cancel out the challenges.

A successful family business transition usually requires several years of pre-planning before the transition can be completed. Additionally, several classes of assets are created so the selling owner can have financial independence without putting undue strain on the core business. This might include the selling owner purchasing and continuing to own the real estate the business operates at, and/or the creation and funding a high-level qualified retirement plan that can provide income after the selling owner stops work. In some cases, current tax law motivates the way the business is sold. Most selling owners prefer to minimize taxes, so it becomes easier for their offspring to afford the purchase of the business.

> If you are contemplating selling your business to family members, it is important to understand the following issues: economic and financial independence issues, family dynamics, corporate governance and how many mouths the business can feed.

As with all business liquidity events, careful consideration must be a part of the transition. In many instances the selling owners will be owed a large amount of money over a long period of time. A financial plan that provides a roadmap showing what the senior generation economic situation looks like is a necessary step in planning a family business transition. Most senior generation business owners are not willing to part with ownership until they know they can economically afford to do so. Typically, a wealth transfer conversation occurs concurrently with the economic transition. Most owners of family businesses want to see all of their children treated fairly. This means the parents should deal with issues of fairness as it relates to the economic value of the business. Combining transition conversations with wealth transfer strategies often lead to solutions that allow the senior generation, the children running the business and the children not in the business to all enjoy an economic outcome that is as fair as possible.

Corporate governance issues become an important area of concentration. The governance issues allow rules of the game to be established for control and for the decision-making processes within the business. The younger generation expects its chance at decision-making, while at the same time the senior generation wants to make sure the nest egg is treated with appropriate stewardship.

The good news about a family business transition is that the nature of the transaction allows the senior generation to make a gentle move from active management to passive management to whatever comes after that. There are best practices for transferring a family business both from an economic and psychological point of view. Some protocols that can make a family business transition more successful include:

- Having a financial plan established. This plan should show where living money will come from once the elder generation stops participating in the family business.

- Having a clear understanding about who can own stock in the family business.

- The establishment of work rules and a family constitution for who can work in the family business and under what circumstances. This should include compensation guidelines for who should get paid for what they do in the business.

- Wealth transfer planning that takes into account the interests of all family stakeholders.

- Rules and protocols for passing control of the family business to the younger generation.

- A requirement for corporate financial performance before control is passed to the younger generation. Having corporate covenants as a pre-condition for passing control of the business is a strong way to protect the interest of the selling generation.

- Strategies that allow the junior generation to run the business while protecting the financial interest of the senior generation. A third-party mediator can be an important member of the transition team while these protocols are developed.

- An understanding by the junior generation that the seniors will participate in strategic decisions about the family business. Again, a third-party mediator can be extremely helpful.

- The establishment of formal business structures, such as a board of directors and family councils, to keep family issues around the family and business issues around the business.

Family business protocols are significant and complicated. Once family dynamics, as well as transition strategies, are brought to the table, conflicts can arise. Having a formal methodology in place for dealing with these possibilities often spells the difference between success and failure.

If you are the parent in a family business transfer, chances are that a classic liquidity event is not likely. As in the internal transition, wealth coaching for putting money aside for later use is essential. Strong financial blueprinting becomes important during the planning phase of a family business transfer. Budgeting for what can be spent versus what needs to be saved for future living needs is a vital part of the process.

Another consideration when making transition plans involves a large balloon payment on the death of the selling owner. This balloon payment can cause a classic liquidity event for children not involved in the business. Planning for this liquidity event should be part of the entire transition planning process.

Liquidation of the Business

The fourth potential liquidity event is through the actual liquidation of your business. Often, this is a negative event. There are two main types of liquidations:

- Liquidation planned as an integrated exit strategy. For example, some construction companies plan a liquidation event by selling off all of their equipment as a partial method of raising needed money for retirement purposes.

- An unplanned liquidation occurs when an owner decides to leave the business due to health reasons, business problems or burnout. Often, this liquidation event is accompanied by a restructuring of business debt. Usually, the results of this type of liquidation do not have positive results for the selling owner.

Personal financial planning becomes quickly necessary if you are facing an unplanned liquidation. Will you have to get another job to bridge the time between liquidating the business and having the ability to stop working for money? Have you planned for what's next in your life?

Most private business owners dream of selling their business and riding off into the sunset. For those who completely liquidate their businesses — especially in an unplanned manner, this dream may not translate into reality. Under some liquidation strategies, bankruptcy is part of the solution. If this is a possibility, the earlier you contact a bankruptcy attorney, the better your chances of keeping some of the assets you've built. If you have significant creditors, a settlement must be reached with them as part of the liquidation process.

The psychological impact of liquidating a business is similar to the third-party sale in many ways. However, the effects of the liquidation are often more immediate and sudden. When you liquidate your business, there is no option for you to continue working for a period, and no option for you to become a significant part of a purchasing business. Your business ceases to exist the day you close your doors. The supplier, customer, peer and employee relationships you have enjoyed for years fade away. The phone stops ringing and you are faced with finding a way to fill the time that you used to fill by running your business. Some business owners have enough money to stop working, even after liquidation. Others find that another job is necessary to make ends meet. Under either scenario you are likely to experience a rollercoaster-type existence as you get used to a new life without your business.

Business owners are known for building their entire social lives around owning the business. Self-esteem is often linked to owning a business. When you liquidate your business, more than just the company evaporates. There is a real chance for depression to set in. Depression in such circumstances might be based upon the business being liquidated or it might be based upon not knowing what to do next. Having a support system is truly important when your business closes due to an unplanned liquidating event.

The following suggestions can help you when considering a liquidating event:

- Create a cash-flow-based financial plan. Know what your options are and develop plans for financial security after you close the doors of your business.

- Think about engaging the services of an asset protection or bankruptcy lawyer. If your creditors take all of the money you receive from liquidation, you may have nothing to fall back on.

- Have a support system in place for helping you through the transition from the business owner role.

- If possible, plan for a liquidating event before it happens. It is prudent to consider the largest dangers facing your personal financial life. If liquidation is one of them, having a plan in place before a liquidating event can help you know what to do while your personal confidence recovers.

Most business owners classify liquidation as the least favorite way of leaving their businesses. Unfortunately, liquidation happens more than is necessary. Spend some time developing your management team, and/or finding a successor, years before you are ready to leave your business. Such measures can forestall liquidation altogether.

Conclusion

For a business owner, the transition from running a company to becoming a retiree is a big one. Understand your options and develop strategies for successful transition implementation well ahead of time. The sale of your business is something you can — and should — plan for. Consider assembling a team of professionals who can help you navigate through this time of your life.

- **Wealth Manager**: This person coordinates your transition team as well as your transition. He or she is responsible for helping you choose other members of your team and helping you identify and hire specialists for exiting your business. Your wealth manager must be able to think about your situation in a comprehensive manner and have a history of working collaboratively with other advisors in bringing about a positive outcome. A wealth manager who specializes in working with private business owners can help you gain clarity about how you want to exit your business, plan the specific strategies for the exit, implement the strategies with appropriate help and work with you through transitions as the years unfold after you sell your business.

- **Accountant**: This person should understand the financial and tax implications of the various liquidity options. He or she should be able to communicate the various tax advantages of leaving your business one way versus another way. The accountant should be able to communicate effectively about the sub-methods of leaving a business. For example, if you are completing an internal transaction, you want your accountant to be able to discuss tax-advantaged internal sales, leveraged buyouts and ESOPs.

- **Transaction attorney**: Your attorney should have experience with a variety of business exit strategies. He or she should be experienced in internal transactions, external transactions and liquidating events. Your attorney should be willing to bring in outside expertise to augment the team, if his or her knowledge is incomplete in any area.

- **Estate planning attorney**: An estate attorney can help you understand business transactions and how they affect estate and wealth transfer planning. Before moving forward with any planning, you must have a clear understanding of what you are trying to accomplish. Start with a temporary plan. As you become more comfortable with your new situation, you can begin to make decisions that are irrevocable and have long-range results.

- **Financial planner**: In many cases, this team member is also your wealth manager. A financial planner must be able to work with you on cash flow-based planning decisions about your exit strategies from the business. He or she must understand private business ownership and have the ability to integrate the needs of you as a business owner with you as an individual. Experience helping business owners successfully navigate planning needs during times of transition is also desirable.

- **Business intermediary**: This person can be a business broker, mergers and acquisition advisor or investment banker. Since there are few intermediaries who have experience in all areas of business transition, it can be helpful to add this member of the team after you decide which method of transferring your business works best for you.

Other professionals who can help you in planning and managing your liquidity event include investment advisors, insurance professionals, family business consultants and psychologists. Your wealth manager should help you decide whether extra help is needed — and be able to identify competent people from across the country to contribute to the process.

Planning for your liquidity event is a complicated process. It makes sense to put together a team that understands your needs and has the technical ability to produce positives result for your specific financial and psychological situation.

◆◆◆

Josh Patrick, CFP®, Principal
Stage 2 Planning Partners
20 Kimball Avenue, Ste. 201
South Burlington, VT 05403
Tel: 802.846.1264
Fax: 802.846.1269
Email: jpatrick@stage2planning.com

http://www.stage2planning.com
http://www.stage2solutions.com

ABOUT THE AUTHOR: Josh Patrick, President of The Patrick Group has spent his adult life running and building businesses. For the first 20 years of his business career, he was President and operated Patrick's Food Service. From a company with one employee Josh built the company to four branch operations with 90 employees.

During Josh's tenure in the food service business he served as President of the New York State Vending Association, was Education Director for the National Vending Association and in that capacity developed several courses on Financial and People Management skills. He currently writes a bi-monthly column on maintaining financial wealth for several industry magazines.

In 1995 he sold his vending operation and started working in the financial services industry. First, for a large Mutual Insurance Company and since 1997 as Principal of his own firm Stage 2 Planning Partners.

Josh specializes in working with closely held business owners on a variety of cocentrated issues that are unique to owners of private firms. Among these arrisk assessment, cash flow planning, investment planning, retirement plan dsign, estate planning, succession planning and family business strategies.

Josh has a belief that integrated planning through a total wealth management approach is the only effective way for owners of private businesses to achieve their personal and financial goals. He and his team have developed a suite of tools that help the private business owner first understand what is important for the owner and then what strategies can deliver the wanted results.

Josh has spoken for many national trade associations and specializes in helping owners of closely held businesses develop plans that improve their personal satisfaction and bottom line in their business. His platform speeches concentrate on giving attendees true take-home value from the programs that they can implement on their return to their office.

8. Preserving Your Nest Egg After You've Built It

Bob Kargenian
TABR Capital Management, LLC

Congratulations! You have succeeded. Against incredible odds, and with great effort, skill and tenacity, you have created a valuable business. Now comes the tricky bit: the transition. When a small business owner sells his or her business, the transaction often represents the biggest liquidity event in the owner's lifetime. But the actions taken to make him or her successful (and helped to create the big lump sum of cash in the first place), are the exact opposite of what will preserve the capital from the sale of a business over a long period of time — perhaps beyond retirement.

The first section of this chapter discusses the three most common mistakes owners make when they sell their businesses: Lack of Patience, Re-investing in Areas You Know Little or Nothing About, and Failure to Delegate.

Lack of Patience

Many small business owners fall into the Type A personality camp: impatient, excessively time-conscious, insecure about their status, highly competitive, hostile and aggressive, and incapable of relaxation. Some of these characteristics are common among high achievers, but they're not always positive attributes in every situation.

Type A personality executives are often high-achieving workaholics who multi-task, drive themselves with deadlines, and are unhappy about the smallest of delays. If you've just sold your business for a princely sum, it's likely you feel you're getting fair value (we're not addressing distress sales here). Though it is very difficult to do, long-term successful investors buy when everyone else is selling, and sell when everyone else is buying. Patience is required — and sometimes delays are inevitable.

Like common stocks, real estate and private equity, most businesses go through stages of over- and under-valuation, so it's important to have patience when re-deploying your capital. Take the time to assess your life and your goals, and make sure you have a plan in place. There is much truth to this saying:

> *"If you don't know where you're going,*
> *how will you know when you get there?"*

For example: If you made a private equity investment yielding 8% return and the same investment is now selling with the yield at 5%, it's not likely you're going to find a lot of bargains left in that type of asset. Sometimes, depending on where things are in the cycle, sitting on cash for a while can be the best decision. If you are a Type A personality, you may have to restrain yourself. In your present situation time is an ally, not an enemy.

Stay Within Your Expertise

Retirement, of course, is not the only option when a small business owner sells out. Many small business owners buy and sell several companies during their careers. In addition to the above-mentioned character traits, many Type A personality executives tend toward arrogance. There is a fine line between arrogance and confidence in successful individuals.

Arrogance can lead one to think, "If I can manage this business, I can manage any business." That is a very risky assumption. Some traits regarding running a successful business ARE transferable. Having proper financial controls or an understanding of balance sheets, debt, revenue and expenses are items that can serve you in any business venture. But not all businesses are alike. Having success in one industry does not automatically translate to other industries. All in all, it is best to stick to your own knitting — that is, stick to what you know. If you choose to go outside your area of expertise, make sure you have experienced people in place who are familiar with the industry.

Failure to Delegate

This might be the hardest thing of all for a Type A personality business owner. After all, he or she was primarily responsible for the success of the business just sold, so why hand the reins to someone else?

Again, the secret is recognizing what you know, and what you don't. For example, managing your own money is not the same as managing your own business. In fact, it is one of the hardest things to do successfully, but you won't read about that in *Smart Money* or *The Wall Street Journal*. Instead, the print media have perpetrated a myth that with a computer, the Internet, a brokerage account and a few keystrokes, you, too, can be the master of your own portfolio. Consider, would you do brain surgery on yourself after studying Wikipedia?

Focus, Leverage and Concentration

There are those who say, "Put all your eggs in one basket, and then watch that basket." Many entrepreneurs have done just that, and created very successful companies. But when it comes to investing a large lump sum of capital that they plan to live on the rest of their lives, putting all their eggs in one basket could be a recipe

Know What You Don't Know

A great example of a successful business owner striking out in an area he knows nothing about is Daniel Snyder, the owner of the NFL's Washington Redskins. Snyder sold his firm, Snyder Communications, for in excess of $2 billion to Havas Advertising, the second largest advertising agency in France. Obviously, he had built a successful business. With part of those proceeds, he purchased the Redskins, once a proud, successful franchise under the late Jack Kent Cooke.

Under Snyder's ownership and incessant meddling, the team has had five head coaches in the past nine years and is considered one of the worst-run franchises in the league. How successful do you think any company would be if they had five CEO's in nine years? Snyder's failure has been in not hiring competent football people and then staying out of the way. ◆

for disaster. It is a risk that is simply too great.

This section will focus on the psychological differences between successful business owners and competent investors. Do you have the skill set to make a successful transition from business owner to competent investor?

The focus, leverage and concentration that got you here, is not likely to keep you here. Many investors — employees and shareholders alike — have made fortunes in their company stock. Many have also lost fortunes in those very same companies. Many of the most successful have cashed out along the way and diversified. Even the greatest names become too big and things change. Consider Microsoft and Starbucks, two of the most recognizable names in America (if not the world). Look at Charts #1 and #2.

From 1996 to 2000, Microsoft shares surged from $7 to $59, a gain of over 800%. In the fall of 2008, they were around $26, after hitting $22 in 2002. That's a 62% decline from the peak and eight years of "dead" money. Likewise, Starbucks rewarded shareholders with an 800% gain, moving from $5 in 1999 to $40 in 2007. In the fall of 2008, these shares were just below $15, a 62% drop from the peak.

Since 1970, the U.S. stock market has dropped 40% from its peak three times (1972-1974, 2000-2002 and 2007-2008). Real estate in many areas of the U.S. has dropped at least 20% from its peak twice since 1990 (1991-1994 and 2005 to the present). Having all of your assets in either of these areas, especially in one's retirement account, would be like running through a dynamite factory with a match. You might live, but you're still an idiot.

The Importance of Minimizing Downside Volatility

You need to become concerned about risk when most other investors become convinced that it does not exist. There are certainly times when it appears easy, in hindsight, to make money in the stock market. When the stock market is rising, everyone's a star investor. The difficulty is keeping your money through a full stock market cycle. The fact that over half of most bull market advances are surrendered in a subsequent bear market doesn't sink in until after the fact.

"It's all fun and games until someone gets hurt."

Those are the words of John P. Hussman, PhD, portfolio manager of the Hussman Strategic Growth Fund, in his February 5, 2007 weekly market

Chart #1

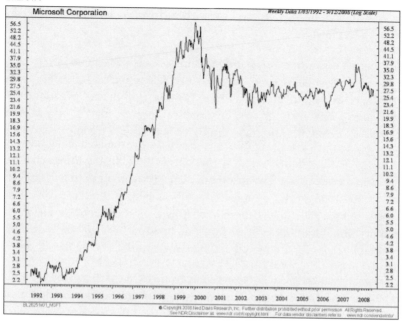

Chart #2

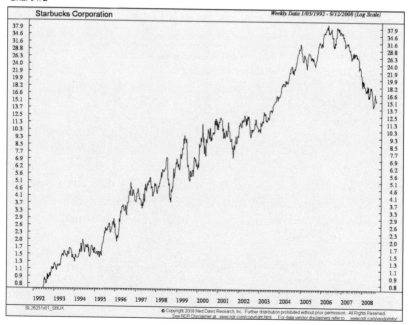

comment. If you've just garnered a lump sum from the sale of your business, and your family needs to live off the income from your portfolio, you can't afford to "get hurt."

This doesn't mean that you shouldn't take risk with the capital that you've created. It is essential that a prudent investor take some risk in order to keep up with, or exceed, inflation over time. So what do I mean by "get hurt?" I mean losing 30%, 40%, or 50% or more in the stock market or any other asset class, including real estate, through poor risk management, excessive leverage or a lack of diversification.

Stocks, as an asset class, have lost more than 45% from peak to trough three times since 1968 — during the 1968-74 bear market, the 2000-2002 bear market, and the 2007-2008 bear market. This section will concentrate on explaining, through examples, that how one does in the "bad" times is more important to a successful retirement than how one does in the "good" times.

Chart #3 shows the year-by-year values from 1970 through 1999 of a hypothetical $100,000 investment covered by a technical risk management strategy and the S&P 500 Index. As you can see, the total return of each investment at the end of 1999 was nearly identical—13.5% compounded vs. 13.72% for the S&P 500 Index. For the buy-and-hold investor, there wasn't much difference. Until you look under the hood.

Chart #3

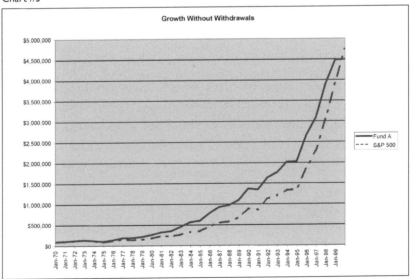

In Chart #4 I've illustrated the same two investments, with one difference. In this example, I've assumed the small business owner takes the lump sum of $1 million from the sale of his business, and starts monthly withdrawals using an annual rate of 5%. Beginning in year two, the withdrawals are increased by 5% each year thereafter to account for inflation, which happens to increase at slightly above this rate during the period, as measured by the Consumer Price Index (CPI).

Chart #4

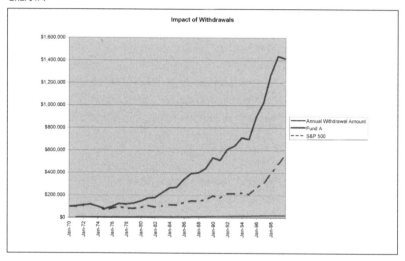

The end result is that an investor withdraws the same amount of money using each strategy; but, when using the first strategy the end value is more than double that of investing in the S&P 500 Index. Why is that?

It comes down to lower downside volatility and the mathematics of recovery. First, when a diversified portfolio is in income mode, it is a fact of life that in certain years, the portfolio will lose money on top of the amount withdrawn. The key is not withdrawing so much that you run the risk of ruin over the longer term.

In this example, the S&P 500 strategy for income suffered a 44% loss of principal during the 1973-74 bear market. In contrast, the investor using the risk management strategy lost 34% of the invested capital. Later, in 1981, the S&P 500 strategy *lost* over 12% while the risk management strategy *gained* more than 2%. Consistently, over time, the risk management strategy lost less in the down periods than the S&P 500 strategy. When you lose less, you retain more of your initial capital. When you lose more, it is much harder to work your way back to even.

Chart #5

The Mathematics of Recovery	
Amount Lost	% Gain Needed to Recover
20%	25%
33%	50%
50%	100%

There are a lot of money managers and strategies that post impressive numbers when the market is going up, but what good is that approach if most, or all, of the gains are given back in a bear market?

Down-Market Cycles/Secular Bear Markets

Wall Street, many of its advisors, and many members of the media emphasize that since 1926, large company stocks as represented by the S&P 500 have compounded at about 10.5% annually. While this is a true statement, it tends to be used in the context of conveying that, in the long run, stocks have provided the greatest inflation-adjusted return of any asset class.

Unfortunately, that statement can also be as useless as stating that Charles Manson is a man. In both cases, there is more to the story, especially when it comes to income planning after the sale of one's hard-won business. The additional story becomes increasingly important when one considers that the typical business seller is looking at a time period for retirement that may easily encompass 20 to 30 years.

Stock returns move in cycles, tied to valuations. In the 1980s and 1990s, large company stocks compounded at more than 17% annually. But many people, investors and advisors alike, either didn't know or didn't remember that the 1960s and 1970s were quite different. As the table on page 119 illustrates, large company stocks compounded at around 6% to 8% in the 1960s and 1970s.

More specifically, in the period from 1966 to 1981, when the Dow Jones Industrial Average went from 1000 to below 800 (not counting dividends), large company stocks (as measured by the S&P 500 Index) compounded at 5.94% during this 16-year period.

This decade, beginning in 2000, is shaping up to be the worst decade for large company stocks in the U.S. since the Depression era. The over-valuation of technology stocks and other Internet-related issues created a bubble whose bursting is still being felt.

Chart #6

Compound Annual Rates of Return by Decade (in percent)***									
	1920s*	1930s	1940s	1950s	1960s	1970s	1980s	1990s	2000s**
Large Company	19.2	-0.1	9.2	19.4	7.8	5.9	17.5	18.2	1.7
Small Company	-4.5	1.4	20.7	16.9	15.5	11.5	15.8	15.1	10.8
Long-Term Corporate	5.2	6.9	2.7	1.0	1.7	6.2	13.0	8.4	8.1
Long-Term Government	5.0	4.9	3.2	-0.1	1.4	5.5	12.6	8.8	8.8
Intermediate-Term Government	4.2	4.6	1.8	1.3	3.5	7.0	11.9	7.2	6.4
Treasury Bills	3.7	0.6	0.4	1.9	3.9	6.3	8.9	4.9	3.2
Inflation	-1.1	-2.0	5.4	2.2	2.5	7.4	5.1	2.9	2.8

*Based on the period 1928-1929
**Based on the period 2000-2007
***Data from 2005 Ibbotson SBBI Classic Yearbook

In contrast, small company stocks have posted fairly consistent returns over time, although they tend to exhibit much more volatility. All in all, it is rarely a prudent risk to fall in love with an asset class and place a majority of one's capital in a single area — especially after one has sold his or her business for a large sum and is depending on the capital to generate retirement income. Be humble. Diversify.

The chart above shows that the time period of the 1960s to 1970s was very similar to what happened recently, from 2000 to 2008.

The Solution

Diversify, diversify, diversify. If one asked the question, "What is the single most important thing to remember when it comes to preserving one's nest egg?" the answer is DIVERSIFY. To do this you just need to follow two simple rules.

Rule # 1

Diversify your capital into several asset classes:

- Stocks (large, mid-sized, small, international, sectors)

- Bonds (short-term, long-term, high-yield, foreign, government)

- Real Estate (liquid forms such as real estate investment trusts or REITS)

- Commodities

Rule # 2

Remember Rule # 1

As noted earlier, since 1970 there have been three bear market periods in which large or small company stocks (or both) have declined more than 40% from peak to trough. The first bear market occurred from 1968 to 1974, the second from 2000 to 2002, and the third from 2007 to 2008.

In the first period, an all-stock allocation lost in excess of 42% in 1969-70 in small company stocks, and more than 50% in the 1973-74 period. In the latter period, large company stocks fell more than 41%. These kinds of losses can ruin a portfolio in retirement, causing one to run out of money prematurely. In fact, losses of these types would be devastating even for an investor not withdrawing capital for income.

In the second period, from 2000 to 2002, large company stocks fell more than 42%. But, as both tables show, by simply diversifying into intermediate bonds, both a moderate and conservative investor could have withstood both periods reasonably well, and significantly enhanced the probabilities that they would not run out of money.

During the period 1968-1974 (see chart below), a moderate risk account, defined as having 40% in large stocks, 20% in small stocks and 40% in bonds, would have lost about 4% in 1969-70 and about 23% in 1973-74. A conservative account, defined as having 25% in large stocks, 15% in small stocks and 60% in bonds, would have gained about 2% in 1969-70, and lost about 12% in 1973-74.

Chart #7

1968 - 1974 DOWN MARKET CYCLE					
YEAR	LARGE CAP*	SMALL CAP**	INTERMEDIATE BOND***	Moderate 40L/20S/40B	Conservative 25L/15S/60B
1969	-8.50	-25.05	-0.74	-8.71	-6.33
1970	4.01	-17.43	16.86	4.86	8.50
1971	14.31	16.50	8.72	12.51	11.28
1972	18.98	4.43	5.16	10.54	8.51
1973	-14.66	-30.90	4.61	-10.20	-5.53
1974	-26.47	-19.95	5.69	-12.30	-6.20

*Large Cap as measured by S&P 500 Total Returns
**Small Cap as measured by Ibbotson Small Company Index
***As measured by Ibbotson Intermediate Government Bond Index

In the bear market from 2000-2002 (see Chart #8, page 121), a moderate risk account as defined above would have lost about 11%, while a conservative account actually would have gained just under 3%. This was a very unusual period, as at the end of 1999, small companies were extremely under-valued in comparison with large companies, and interest rates were relatively high. Just by having the diversification of small companies and bonds, one would have survived relatively unscathed in a period that was quite traumatic for many investors.

Chart #8

	LARGE CAP*	SMALL CAP**	TOTAL BOND***	Moderate 40L/20S/40B	Conservative 25L/15S/60B
2000-2002 BEAR MARKET					
2000	-9.11	-2.67	11.39	0.40	4.17
2001	-12.02	3.10	8.43	-0.82	2.52
2002	-22.15	-20.02	8.26	-9.56	-3.57

*Large Cap as measured by S&P 500 Total Return
**Small Cap as measured by Vanguard Small Cap Index Fund, Symbol NAESX
***As measured by the Vanguard Total Bond Index, Symbol VBMFX

It is widely accepted today that even further diversification can take place by including international equities, real estate in the form of liquid real estate investment trusts (REITS), and commodities in one's portfolio. That information, with further enhancements by weighting the various asset classes by relative strength, is beyond the scope of this chapter, but the main message is this:

Diversification works over time.

Risk Management

Let's take a look at modern risk management techniques: What are they? Where can they be found? How they can be used effectively? Additionally, gold as an investment will be discussed.

If you enter the term "risk management definition" in your Google search engine, one of the results is "the process of analyzing exposure to risk and determining how to best handle such exposure." For our use, risk management is the process and/or techniques used to help minimize downside volatility in a portfolio.

As you may have gleaned from the previous section, diversification is one form of risk management. By adding bonds to an all-stock portfolio, a significant reduction in risk is attained. With the creation in the last decade of inverse funds and exchange-traded funds (ETFs), both leveraged and unleveraged, a number of tools, previously unavailable to investors, exist today to hedge portfolios. Hedging is a strategy that attempts to reduce the risk of a portfolio by making investments that are expected to perform differently than — or even offset — each other.

Inverse funds are mutual funds or ETFs that aim to act as short positions. For example, if the index targeted declines 1%, the inverse fund increases in value by 1%. ETFs are index funds or trusts that listed on an exchange and traded in a similar fashion to a single equity or common stock.

For instance, inverse funds may be appropriate when you want to hedge— to lessen the impact of a market decline, but you don't want to sell. Today, inverse funds and ETFs exist not only on broad stock market indexes, but also on specific industries (technology, energy, real estate, etc.) and on commodities (gold, oil).

In the past, gold and real estate have tended to non-correlate with stocks and bonds, their inclusion in a portfolio potentially smoothing returns over time. In addition, relative strength techniques are a great risk management tool. "Relative strength" is a term used by technical analysts to evaluate how a stock or index is performing in comparison to another group of stocks, indexes or funds. In other words, it measures relative performance rather than absolute performance.

Though many financial advisors may advocate static portfolio weightings, such as 40% bonds, 40% large stocks and 20% small stocks, a relative strength approach would look to over-weight large stocks or small stocks in relation to each other, depending on which is doing better, based on an unemotional, back-tested mathematical formula. Over time, this form of risk management can significantly add to the bottom line of a portfolio.

When Will Your Savings Run Out? Spending Rules After the Sale

This section focuses on "the percentage." It is a very different dynamic living off one's income as compared to living off one's earnings. People begin to think differently about their money because they may no longer be "earning" a paycheck. The big question becomes this:

"What percentage of my account can I safely withdraw on an annual basis and still keep my principal intact?"

"The percentage" is not always the issue for every business seller. Some small business owners are concerned with passing funds on to their heirs, while others may not view providing an inheritance as a priority. Perhaps another way to ask this question is this:

"What percentage can I withdraw so that I don't outlive my money?"

The answers depend on four factors, only two of which we can fully control. Those factors are:

1. Your withdrawal rate (or how much are you spending)

2. What return your portfolio earns

3. When you retire

4. How long you live

Obviously, the higher return on your investments, the more money you can take out, but we don't know what the markets are going to do during the next 10 or 20 years. At least not for sure, though there are credible ways to forecast this with some degree of accuracy. However, being conservative with your withdrawal rate is the prudent course of action if you are concerned about preserving your principal.

For our example, we assume that it is important for the seller to maintain his or her principal, and that the money needs to last 30 years. Most people retire at age 60 or later, but there are certainly some who choose to, or have the option to, retire in their 50s. Today, actuarial tables indicate that 65-year-old males and females have life expectancies of about 82 and 85 years, respectively. But one should note there is an 18.4% probability that at least one member of a 65-year-old couple will live at least 30 years.

A number of exhaustive studies have been done on the subject of appropriate withdrawal rates for portfolios in retirement. Two of the more credible pieces of work are authored by William P. Bengen[1] and Jonathan Guyton[2]. Both conclude that "safe" withdrawal rates range between 4.5% and 5.5% of capital. "Safe" means that if one sticks to a particular rate between these ranges, in combination with a diversified portfolio, the probabilities of running out of money over a 30-year time period are extremely low.

On the next page is a simple matrix (Chart #9) which combines various withdrawal rates with various savings growth rates. For instance, if one uses a 5% withdrawal rate, but the portfolio returned only 4% over time, the money still lasts 41 years. With a 6% withdrawal rate combined with 5% earnings, that same money lasts 37 years. With the low return environment of the past nine years possibly extending for another decade, it is important than an investor not spend too much capital if preservation of principal is an important goal.

1 Conserving Client Portfolios During Retirement (2006)
2 Decision Rules and Portfolio Management for Retirees (FPA Journal 2004)

The chart can help you estimate the number of years your current savings may last. Plot the number of years remaining by picking your savings growth rate and your rate of withdrawal (the chart assumes that you DO NOT add to your savings).

Chart #9

Growth Rate	2%	3%	4%	5%	6%	7%	8%	9%	10%	11%	12%
10%										25	19
9%									27	20	16
8%								29	21	17	14
7%							31	22	18	15	13
6%						33	24	19	16	14	12
5%					37	26	20	17	14	12	11
4%				41	28	22	18	15	13	12	10
3%			47	31	23	19	16	14	12	11	10
2%		55	35	26	20	17	15	13	11	10	9
1%	70	41	29	22	18	15	13	12	11	10	9

NOTE: The table shows a conservative withdrawal rate and how it can preserve principal over time.

Long-Term Equity and Fixed Income Returns

This section will concentrate on illustrating the future for small business owners. It is not necessary to forecast the future to properly design an income plan for small business owners faced with the largest liquidity event of their lives. But expectations are a critical part of investor behavior, and a realistic look based on prudent historical research might prove quite helpful in answering the question: "What can I expect from here, in 2008/2009?"

One of the more common methods of determining valuation methods in the stock market is to divide the price of a stock by the earnings of the stock, producing what is known as the price/earnings ratio (P/E). This same approach can be used to assess the valuation of a stock market index, or the broader market.

In general, periods beginning with low P/E ratios produce subsequent above-average returns, while periods beginning with high P/E ratios produce subsequent below-average returns. This is due mostly to the expansion or contraction in the trend of P/E ratios, coupled with the dividend yield.

Though many advisors in the industry often quote that the long-term return on stocks since 1926 is about 10.5%, this is of little use to an investor with a 20- to 30-year time horizon. As shown above, there are long periods of time, even decades, when stocks produce below-average returns.

In the late 1990s, P/E ratios surged well above the 20 level. This presaged below-average future returns, according to research from Ed Easterling at Crestmont Research. The chart below, from Easterling's website, www.CrestmontResearch.com, breaks the P/E ratio for the S&P 500 into deciles, going back to 1919, then computes forward 20-year compound returns from each beginning data point.

Chart #10

	20 Year Period Ending 1919-2007 (89 periods)				
	NET TOTAL RETURNS BY DECILE RANGE		S&P 500 DECILE	AVG BEGIN	AVG END
DECILE	FROM	TO	AVG	P/E	P/E
1	1.2%	4.5%	3.2%	19	9
2	4.5%	5.2%	4.9%	18	9
3	5.2%	5.4%	5.3%	12	12
4	5.4%	6.0%	5.6%	13	12
5	6.2%	7.9%	7.0%	15	15
6	8.0%	9.0%	8.7%	16	19
7	9.0%	9.6%	9.3%	15	19
8	9.7%	11.0%	10.4%	11	20
9	11.5%	11.9%	11.7%	12	22
10	12.1%	15.0%	13.4%	10	29

Note: P/E ratio based upon Shiller methodology

Copyright 2003-2008, Crestmont Research (www.crestmontresearch.com)

At the end of 1999, the P/E ratio for the S&P 500 was in the first decile. In the past, net total returns from this decile have ranged from 1.2% to 4.5%, with an average of 3.2%. As of June 30, 2008, eight and one-half years into this decade, the compound return of the Vanguard Total Stock Market Index has been 0.8%, while the Vanguard Small Cap Stock Index Fund has gained 5.8% per annum.

The median P/E ratio continues to be near the 17 level, placing it in the second decile, where past returns have ranged from 4.5% to 5.2%. A slightly different methodology employed by Dr. John Hussman (www.hussmanfunds.com) suggests that the most likely 10-year return for the S&P 500 from current levels (900) is now in the range of 7% to 11%.

With yields on Treasury Notes at 4% and yields on corporate bonds and global bonds in the 7% to 9% range, it would be imprudent to suggest that fixed income allocations for the next 10 years could yield much more than this, without a substantial jump in yields. Coupled with reasonable expectations from equities in the 7% to 11% range, investors with diversified portfolios should be prepared for 10-year future returns in the 6-8% compound range.

Summary

In this chapter, we discussed the three most common mistakes made by owners when they sell their businesses:

- Lack of patience

- Reinvesting in areas without a knowledge base

- Failure to delegate

We also learned how focus, leverage and concentration can be the enemy of the small business owner after the sale, and why minimizing downside volatility in a retirement income stream is critical to the long-term viability of the plan.

We learned that stocks, for very long periods of time, can produce below-average returns, and that the solutions for getting through these difficult periods are diversification and risk management. Finally, we touched on the most appropriate withdrawal rates for income portfolios and what to expect in the way of future returns for the next 10 years.

In closing, I want to tell the true story about a small business owner who sold his company in 1995 at the age of 67. At that time, he retired in the traditional sense, and had plenty of capital to live a comfortable life with his wife, enjoying his children and grandchildren. But the story does not end there. In the past 13 years, he has made two significant investments in private equity transactions, with the first yielding more than an 8-1 return over eight years and the second paying more than 5-1 in five years.

The first transaction was in an industry he knew quite well. In the second transaction, he relied upon outside expertise in an area he had no experience in. In other words, he diversified and delegated, and even today at 80 years old, he is looking for appropriate opportunities. Long ago, he made the successful transition from small business owner to competent investor. It can be done as long as you pay attention, recognizing both your areas of strength and areas where you can use others' expertise, just like you did to achieve your current success.

◆◆◆

Bob Kargenian, President
TABR Capital Management, LLC
500 N. State College Blvd., Ste 1320
Orange, CA 92868
Tel: 714.704.9180
Email: bkargenian@tabr.net
http://www.tabr.net

ABOUT THE AUTHOR: Robert (Bob) Kargenian founded the fee-only financial advisory firm TABR Capital Management, LLC in January 2004. Bob has a wealth of experience in the financial services industry, having been active in financial planning for more than 20 years. He and his colleagues at TABR manage more than $150 million of personal and client capital on a discretionary basis, using the same tried and true investment strategies for clients as they do for their own personal investments.

Prior to founding TABR, Bob held positions at Prudential Securities, Wachovia Securities and E.F. Hutton & Company.

Bob has been a Chartered Market Technician and Professional Member of the Market Technicians Association since 1989. He is an expert on markets, trading and managing investment risk. He takes a disciplined, risk-management approach to money management, relying on quantitative models for market insight.

His stock market research has appeared in Technical Analysis of Stocks & Commodities as well as in a special report published by Gerald Appel of Signalert Corporation.

He holds a Bachelor of Arts degree in Sports Administration from California State University, Fullerton. Bob is a member of the Paladin Registry, an independent resource for fiduciary investment professionals. He and his wife, Michelle, live with their son and daughter in Yorba Linda, California.

9. Unlock the Power of the Entrepreneurial Imagination

Keith W. Johnson, CFP®

T he mind has a distinct ability that enables us to dream. For most people, dreams are little more than fleeting thoughts, born out of the imagination, that pass through the brain while we sleep. (Although most of us have been known to do a little daydreaming as well.) Some people, however, learn to use the power of their dreams and imagination as a source of inspiration and empowerment. New inventions, new business ideas and innovations to existing businesses and ideas are all products of the power of dreams and imagination. Effective use of the power of your dreams and imagination can also provide the ability to envision such desirables as a perfect world, an ideal marriage, a wonderful family life or a great retirement in some exotic place. People who understand this power also realize that they can use the mind and the imagination to envision such grandiose concepts as achievement, greatness and success.

It is also important to understand that we can create negative ideas with our minds. Through the imagination our minds can manufacture needless fear and doubt — emotions that often hinder our actions. The mind can create imaginary obstacles that inhibit great ideas or leave us immobile. We sometimes afflict ourselves with self-doubt and worry about what might happen without regard to facts or truth. Imagination can produce disbelief that erodes confidence and faith.

Most small businesses are born out of a simple thought, dream or idea. A business usually begins as little more than a mental concept of some marketable idea, invention, product or service. Entrepreneurs are those who rise above doubt and fear and take decisive action to launch a new business venture or market a new idea.

Life Stages of the Business

Once a business is born, it tends to go through several life stages. In its infancy, the business usually struggles for survival. Typically, the new venture depends totally upon its creator. The entrepreneur must fill many roles to make sure that the business is not only launched, but also becomes a viable entity. The owner/creator must carefully control every part of the business to ensure its success.

> Due to the day-to-day pressures of running a growing firm, many small business owners stop dreaming about the future and narrow their focus to the present.

As the business begins to grow and mature past its infancy, it begins to take on a life of its own. Over time, it gradually might evolve into something quite different from what its creator originally envisioned. In many cases, the business begins to manage the entrepreneur rather than the entrepreneur managing the business. It is at this stage that many business owners find their dreaming days numbered.

Due to the day-to-day pressures of running a growing firm, many small business owners stop dreaming about the future and narrow their focus to the present. They concentrate on what must be done just to get through each day and to ensure the business remains viable. Even while sleeping their minds race, filled with thoughts centered on the pressures of that day. Perhaps without even realizing it, these business creators now spend most of their time and energy trying to control and lead the venture they have birthed. Some call it a monster at this point rather than their "baby." Creators often become consumed by their own creations.

Most entrepreneurs realize their business is strong, viable and successful primarily because it has been built upon their own personal strengths and abilities. The owner usually has specific technical expertise in the product or service offered by the entity, meaning he or she is the best expert in the fledgling company. During the early years of a business, it is generally necessary for it to be totally dependent upon the owner. The entrepreneur usually drives the success of the business by retaining tight control over all that happens, with the owner filling many different roles.

Many small business owners believe they have no choice but to manage and control every area of the firm just to ensure its success.

In reality, as the business grows and becomes more established it becomes more difficult to manage every area of the business as effectively as was done during the early years. Unfortunately, many entrepreneurs continue to believe their business will fail without their tight control. Many feel this is essential for the benefit of their clients and customers. They think their clients and customers want it this way.

As the level of complexity grows, and the demands of management become more complicated, many business owners struggle to keep up. Proper administration of the business often takes more hours than anticipated. Pressure builds from the competition. As the business becomes successful, other firms begin to take notice and place it squarely in their sites as the one to beat.

As the business reaches the mature state, many entrepreneurs fight to stay in control and continue to manage every area. Stress and strain begin to take their toll. To help relieve the situation they hire help and try to delegate responsibilities. But, as new employees make mistakes and workflow slows due to lack of experience, many owners react by demanding even tighter control over the business in an effort to make sure everything is done the way it always has been. Soon, they tend to take back areas of responsibility delegated to new employees.

Some business owners begin to suffer both physically and emotionally at this point. Many go through a period of self-doubt, or even depression, as reality sets in. Others experience physical exhaustion from trying to hold it all together. In their efforts to find answers and solutions, some begin to question their own abilities. Some blame their customers and vendors for troubling issues. Others hold their employees responsible for the problems.

This is the point where many business owners start searching for something different. Some look for a new idea or an added line of business. Others seek a new partner or simply sell the business. Another tactic is to suffer through it, working more hours. For the majority, the business simply plateaus and becomes stagnant. In extreme cases profits dry up and the business begins to spiral downward.

The "Mid-Life Crisis" of a Business

When these events occur, your business has reached its mid-life crisis. This is the point at which you must tap into the amazing power of your own brain. Your mind, your imagination, contains amazing power. It allowed you to picture the original creation of your business in the past. It also can enable you to see past the current state of your business and picture a new and better form of it in the future.

> *Calling upon the power of your mind to dream will help you to visualize a re-created ideal business. It will allow you to envision the ideal end game for your life and your business.*

A key to doing this is to separate yourself from the stress and pressure of your business long enough to enable the power of your mind to work for you. Getting away and allowing yourself time to dream and imagine what your business could be like in a better form will open windows of clarity for you. The brightest and best business owners understand that this mid-life crisis can be a turning point for their business. It can actually be the beginning of something far beyond what originally was imagined. In order to build your ideal business, it must become something far more than what it has evolved to at this point. Most owners discover the moment the business is no longer totally dependent upon them for everything. It can takes on a new life and become something far greater. When a business is built around one key person, it is limited to the abilities of that individual. Once the principal of the business learns to let go and enables the firm to function independently, the business finds new life and energy, opening the way for it to operate at a whole new level.

For many entrepreneurs, this progression is very difficult. However, when moving beyond the emotion of change, the business can really start to grow to new heights. Reducing the amount of dependence the business has on you, puts into motion a series of events and circumstances that can result in a much stronger business. It also can generate greater confidence on the part of your clients and customers as they sense that they will be cared for even if you are no longer in the picture. Your customers and clients will view this as a positive change. Their greatest desire is to have you as their product or service provider. Their greatest fear is that if you leave, so will the product or service. Customers and clients expect a contingency plan to be in place, planning for the time when you, personally, will no longer serve them.

Position Your Business for the End Game

The shift in dependence is especially important when preparing for the eventual transition of your business. Most entrepreneurs forget or ignore the fact that sooner or later, one way or another, all businesses transition in some way. Some transition their business in a manner, and at a time, that best meets their own personal goals and objectives. In response to a crisis, others are forced to transition when they least expect to. Still others do not personally experience the transition process during their lifetimes, leaving a mess for others to clean up.

> Preparing for the end game is one of the most important steps a savvy business owner can take.

Preparing for the end game is one of the most important steps a savvy business owner can take. What many do not understand is that the period of preparation for the end game is not just a few years before retirement, but something that should be done early on. Transition can be a wonderful experience, and a stepping-stone to a different level of living. In many cases, proper planning can open the door to new opportunities, enabling you to live out your true life's purpose, rather than spending all your time, energy and money running a business.

Perfect Execution, Greatness and Success

One of the keys for the savvy business owner who wants to grow to new levels of success is to stop what you are doing and take some time away to focus *on* the business, rather than just always working *in* the business. In order for this to be effective, you must tap into the power of your mind. With the influence of the imagination, envision true GREATNESS and SUCCESS for your business and your life.

Most entrepreneurs allow their business to take them on a journey through life rather than managing their business with purpose. They do not realize that a clear and concise plan clarifies where the business will go and what the end game will be. In order to work toward perfect execution, true greatness and success, you must start with new thoughts, bigger dreams and greater imagination.

Savvy business owners learn to take the time to go through a process that helps them imagine and define what greatness and success really are for them and their business. Going through this process will better equip you to take your business and personal life far beyond where it has gone up to now. To help you get started, take a moment to do a brief exercise using the power of imagination:

1. Close your eyes and think back to where it all began. Try to take your mind back to the earliest days of your business. Better yet, think of the months before you actually opened the doors. Remember what it felt like to dream and envision what it would be like to open your own business. Feel the emotions of excitement, anticipation and fear you had. Think back to the many hours each day spent dreaming and thinking about your business. Take a few minutes and write down what you saw and felt.

2. Next, take your mind to a point several years later. What consumed your thoughts at this point? Did you dream about what could be, or did you focus your thoughts on how to get through each day? What were your emotions? Write down what consumed you, and how you felt.

3. Finally, peer into the future. Define what true greatness and success looks like for your business.

Your brain has the wonderful capacity to look into the past and remember all you have experienced. Your mind has recorded every thought, action and emotion. It also has the amazing ability to view the future through the power of imagination. The secret for the savvy business owner is to tap into these amazing abilities of the mind. You want to remember the lessons learned during the journey to date and appreciate the level of success you have already achieved. Perhaps your journey has already taken you far beyond that which you originally imagined. But has your business become all that it can be? Have you become all you can be?

You Are an Ironman!

It is a privilege for me to live in the small community of Kailua-Kona on the beautiful Big Island of Hawaii. Every October the Ironman World Championship takes place on the island. It is an amazing event to see. The athletes go through a series of events in one day: a 2.4 mile swim in the ocean followed by a 112-mile bike race and culminating in a marathon run of 26.2 miles. The men and women who compete at the highest level complete all of this in 10 hours or less.

Most of us can only imagine what it would take to prepare physically for such an event. But beyond the physical preparation, there is also mental preparation. Visualization is used in both professional and Olympic sports to help improve performance. This process allows the athlete to mentally see the entire race or event with flawless execution and perfect results. The athletes picture themselves performing perfectly. They also visualize themselves enjoying the fruits of victory at the end. This process of visualizing both flawless execution and the rewards of success has been shown to significantly improve performance.

Before ever entering the water, top Ironman athletes picture what it will be like to swim the 2.4 miles

in the Pacific Ocean at 7:00 in the morning. They imagine the waves pounding against them, anticipating the feeling of water slapping them in the face as they breathe. They taste the salty water and feel the congestion of all those other swimmers fighting for position around them. They envision perfect execution of each stroke. Next, Ironman athletes imagine the feeling of getting out of the ocean and immediately preparing to jump on their bikes for the 112-mile ride. They reflect on what their skin feels like, anticipating the itching and chafing of riding while wet. In their minds they know the intense heat of the pavement and the lava rock surrounding them as they make their way along that long highway past the airport and beyond the resorts to the very north end of the island. They plan every stop. They picture which stations along the highway will be used to get fruit, water and food. They consider getting a flat tire or worse, falling and badly scraping their arms and legs. These athletes imagine themselves riding back into Kona, where their journey began, and changing their shoes in preparation for the marathon. They physically anticipate the pain lancing through their bodies. They foresee the psychological desire to give up and quit. They feel

Continued on page 136

... continued

the emotions and exhaustion as they get well into their run. But through all of this, one of the most important aspects of visualization for these athletes is to see themselves running down Alii Drive toward the finish line. At this time, they picture the crowds lining the streets to cheer them on. They hear the sounds of helicopters overhead, filled with TV and film crews recording their triumph. In their minds they see their faces on that huge TV screen as they approach the end. They see native Hawaiians standing at the finish line blowing conch shells to announce victory. The exhilaration of crossing the finish line becomes real in the mind's eye. Through visualization, Ironman athletes hear the announcer shouting their names followed by, "YOU ARE AN IRONMAN." They picture their families standing just on the other side of the line, and running into their arms. They mentally see the victory of the end game, before any of it happens in "real life."

Just as visualization is one of the most important parts of the preparation and training process to successfully compete in the Ironman Triathlon World Championship, savvy entrepreneurs learn how to use that same power to visualize their own flawless execution and perfect performance in business. They learn to effectively anticipate the obstacles. They picture solutions to every problem. They feel the emotion of crossing the finish line to enjoy the success of victory. ◆

In order to go to the highest levels of performance, you must use the wisdom gained through years of experience. You must tap into the power of your imagination to dream of far greater things in the future. You must visualize your business and your life operating at levels you never before thought possible. Visualization is a powerful tool that can enable you to increase your own performance. Visualization uses the power of the mind to see perfect performance and execution.

The time is now for you to shift gears in your mind and focus on running your business differently going forward. Now is the time to dream about what should be. It is time to use your brain power to picture a perfect business and see yourself performing at your highest potential. This is your opportunity to reinvent, redefine and redesign your business — and yourself — for the future. Take the time to envision a whole new creation. Use the same brain power that allowed you to create your business to take it to places never before thought possible.

Savvy business owners understand that taking advantage of this opportunity after their business is well established brings even greater value. You are now better equipped to know the true potential of your business. You have already learned many valuable lessons. It is likely that many of these lessons were learned the hard way as you worked through mistakes. Experience really is the greatest teacher. If you leave your mind open to learn, your years of experience can help you visualize the true definition of greatness and success for your business as well as for your life. Your experiences have equipped you to engage the power of your brain to set you on a course that will take your business to new heights, guided by clearer design and greater purpose.

For best results, begin by writing down a formal description of your ideal and perfect business and life. This can be accomplished by preparing a written strategic plan. For some this is a whole new experience. For others, this is an opportunity to dust off the old written business plan prepared years ago. Still others who have gone through a consulting or coaching program may already have a detailed plan. Recognize this opportunity to refine and perfect your plan. Focus on adjusting your plan to make it more meaningful, creating a vital tool to help you run and manage your business with vision and purpose.

Regardless of where you are today, it is important that you take advantage of this opportunity. Go through each step of the process. It will help you to either confirm that your plan is solid and that you are on the right track, or it will point out some important weaknesses and issues that need to be addressed. The strategic planning process will help you redesign and rebuild your business in its ideal and perfect form. A written plan gives definition and purpose to your business. This process represents a vital step for business owners with the desire, drive and determination to take his or her business to the next level.

A good strategic plan provides the foundation upon which every important management decision and every tactical business process is built. As a result, you will achieve very clearly defined results. Your success will not be left up to chance, but rather be the natural result of executing your written plan — a plan based on a clear vision borne out of your dreams and imagination.

4... 3... 2... 1... Start Daydreaming

Think of strategic planning as the process used by many architects to come up with a design concept or sketch. You instinctively went through this process when you were preparing to launch your business. Strategic planning allows you to think, dream and visualize your ideal business. To help you begin, complete this brief exercise:

1. Close your eyes and try to picture your business as it is today. Picture yourself standing outside your facilities. In your mind, walk into the building. Try to objectively look at the layout. See how the building looks to others as they enter. Look at the furnishings and equipment. Write down what you like and dislike.

2. Next, take your mind to the future. What does your ideal business look like? What would your business look like if it were perfect? Imagine how you would feel if you could experience this ideal and perfect business.

3. Think about the end game. What is the greatest conclusion for you and your business? What legacy do you want to leave behind? Write down what you see and what emotions you are feeling.

4. Look at the people in your facility. Are they the right people? Are they doing the right jobs? Are they the individuals best suited to taking your business where it should be?

This exercise is designed to stimulate dreaming and imagining. Once the new concept design is created in your mind, you can begin to write a detailed plan for your business. Strategic Planning is the process of defining the long-term vision and fundamental strategy. It is the process of creating a word picture of exactly what it should look like in its ideal and perfect state without considering any limitations of resources including time, personnel and funding. ◆

Keith W. Johnson, CFP®
P.O. Box 2019
Kailua-Kona HI 96745
Tel: 610.334.1805
Email: keith@krjda.net

ABOUT THE AUTHOR: Keith Johnson has been involved in the financial services industry for more than 25 years. His experience includes the launching of several very successful firms offering financial planning, insurance, income tax preparation and investments. Investment services have been offered through AIG Financial Advisors (AIGFA) since 1985 when he affiliated with the firm as an independent financial advisor and OSJ branch manager.

Keith later sold his successful investment business and Registered Investment Advisor to a community bank holding company in Pennsylvania where he served as President of two subsidiary companies for that firm.

In 2003, he accepted a position as Regional Vice President of AIG Financial Advisors. Shortly thereafter he was promoted to Vice President and became responsible for the successful creation and launch of a newly created Business Development Division. In this role Keith continues to provide leadership over a suite of highly successful coaching and mentoring programs for financial advisors and has authored much of the content. Since their launch in 2005, these programs have contributed significantly to increased success of both the participants and the firm.

His diverse background includes executive leadership in the public company sector as well as investment portfolio management and financial planning in private firms. He also comes with experience in mergers and acquisitions. Keith has served on the board of directors of a public company as well as several private entities and public charities. He is a CERTIFIED FINANCIAL PLANNER™ and holds FINRA Series 7, 8, 63 and 65 securities registrations as well as life, accident, health, property, and casualty insurance licenses.

Keith is a visionary executive, entertaining speaker and motivational leader who inspires and encourages people to initiate positive change and enjoy greatness and success in their life and business.

The 5 Laws: A New Method of Business Transformation

Brett Harward, CEO
Manifest Management Services™

How do businesses succeed? Why do they fail? While the answers to these questions vary on a case-by-case basis and may be anything but simple, they can be grouped to a few very specific laws and principles.

Every problem in business, as well as every success — from profits to productivity, market share to morale, revenues to retirement — are governed by 5 Laws:

1. The Law of Vision
2. The Law of Frequency
3. The Law of Perception
4. The Law of Accountability
5. The Law of Leadership

While these laws may seem simple, often they are not applied by small business owners. They are not a solution in and of themselves, but the basis of an informed method by which business issues may be resolved and foundations laid.

1: The Law of Vision

Vision is what propels forward movement in a company and drives meaning, purpose and innovation. A company's ability to present and articulate a sense of vision clearly to its employees and customers is a determining factor in its chances for growth and success.

An organization that operates without a clear sense of vision, can be recognized by all or some of the following characteristics:

- Employees who spend their days "putting out brush fires," focusing on problems related to the past or attending to duties that ought to have been taken care of by someone else.

- Few opportunities for upward movement among employees, resulting in low morale.

- High employee turnover rates with business leadership regularly working overtime to compensate.
- No perceivable changes in a company's methods or growth over long stretches of time.
- Lack of awareness among business owners at any given time of the company's financial health; unrealistic financial expectations.

A company's shared vision is its life's blood. Vision inspires creativity and presents a consistent backdrop against which any decision in an organization can be tested, measured and weighed.

2: The Law of Frequency

A company's long-term success correlates directly to the amount of time that goes by between the "awareness" and any efforts to take corrective action. The Law of Frequency is vital to a company's well-being, and includes several key components:

- Clear targets, with agreed-upon parameters spanning from unacceptable to outstanding.
- Frequent measurement of results against these same targets.
- Constant and immediate efforts to address discrepancies between targets and results.

Other fundamental elements of fast frequency may take the form of:

- Budgets and appropriate financial reporting.
- Organizational structures and measurements.
- Sales and marketing plans.
- Clearly defined business objectives.
- An honest and consistent employee review system.

Companies who incorporate these elements will see unmistakable — even dramatic — improvements.

3: The Law of Perception

Perception might not be reality, but in the eyes of those who are otherwise unfamiliar with a company, it most certainly is. In business, the prize never goes to the best company or tradesman, but to the one that outsiders see as being the best. The companies that are able to actively manage perceptions are the companies that consistently flourish.

Here are some areas that can create an immediate impact:

- *Offices and office space* — Send a clear signal to customers that you are organized and professional by maintaining office spaces that reflect those values.
- *Paperwork* — Ensure contracts, invoices, correspondence, and other materials are grammatically and numerically correct, and that brand names and logos are clear and consistent. Use a higher-end paper and materials for letterhead and envelopes.
- *People* — Customers are liable to make sweeping assessments of a company's professionalism based on the appearance of its employees. It is important to establish and enforce dress and grooming standings that convey what the company stands for.
- *Vehicles, tools and equipment* — Well cared for vehicles, tools and equipment speak volumes about a company's dependability and attention to details.

The Law of Perception, incidentally, does not apply only to customers. Management, current and potential employee, shareholder, affiliation, and vendor perceptions also are critical to business success.

4: The Law of Accountability

Accountability is the ability to acknowledge what it is that generates a given result. In most organizations, it stems from four primary tools:

- Written policies and procedures.
- Performance-driven position guides or job descriptions.
- Regular employee reviews.
- Compensation, incentive and reward programs that support employee, team and organizational performance.

Accountability starts at the top of any organization and moves down. If leaders, managers, and business owners aren't accountable for anything, then accountability below them can't exist.

5: The Law of Leadership

To work most effectively, the Law of Leadership relies on the first four of the 5 Laws, including:

- The process of communicating vision.
- Execution at a high frequency.

- Recognizing and addressing perceptions.
- Exercising accountability.

The first four laws clearly address structural pillars of successful business practice, such as plans, budgets, job descriptions, and the like. The fifth law is like a rooftop resting upon those four pillars that protects the entire structure from harmful outside forces. It can be broken down into three major areas:

Value — Great leaders recognize people who can either block their progress or assist them in reaching their vision. They have learned to assess the value inherent in their business and interpersonal relationships.

Listening — Great leaders want to know how others feel and how they can create authentic value in relationships -- be they customers, employees, vendors or partners. They practice listening rather than making assumptions or guessing.

Group IQ — Great leaders tap those around them when making decisions. They especially look for input from those who might see things differently than they do. They will consistently make decisions that exceed their own insights and capacity. They understand that harnessing the IQ of the group exponentially increases any individual IQ.

Leadership is a journey that involves constant learning.

The 5 Laws in Practice: A Manifest for Success

Like the Law of Gravity, the 5 Laws for businesses are universal and apply to any business situation. If a heavy object is dropped, the outcome is predictable — it will fall to the ground. Likewise, if a business doesn't put these laws into practice it will underperform. The consistent application of them, on the other hand, will translate directly into growth, productivity, and profitability.

A special thanks to the professionals who contributed chapters and articles to *Financial Savvy for the Small Business Owner*. Contact information for chapter contributors can be found at the end of each individual's chapter. Contact information for article contributors is below.

- **Charles Young, CPA**
  1605 F Street
  PO Box 65381
  Vancouver, WA 98665
  Tel: 360.695.1055
  c.young@charlesyoungcpa.com

- **Josh Patrick, CFP®, Principal**
  Stage 2 Planning Partners
  20 Kimball Avenue, Ste. 201
  South Burlington, VT 05403
  Tel: 802.846.1264
  Fax: 802.846.1269
  Email: jpatrick@stage2planning.com
  http://www.stage2planning.com
  http://www.stage2solutions.com

- **Rafael Pastor, Chairman of the Board & CEO**
  Vistage International, Inc.
  11452 El Camino Real, Suite 400
  San Diego, CA, 92130
  Tel: 858.523.6888
  rafael.pastor@vistage.com
  http://www.vistage.com

- **Brett Harward, CEO**
  Manifest Management Services
  4475 Oxford Way
  Bountiful, UT 84010
  Tel: 801.814.1883 (Chad Harward)
  Email: bharward3@hotmail.com
  http://www.manifestmanagement.com

ADDITIONAL RESOURCES for SMALL BUSINESS OWNERS

The books listed below, and others, can be purchased at Financial Forum Bookstore (www.ffbookstore.com), or by calling 435.750.0062 ext. 4.

- *Absolue Honesty: Building a Corporate Culture that Values Straight Talk and Rewards Integrity* by Larry Johnson & Bob Phillips, List Price: $27.95

- *Baby Boomer Retirement: 65 Simple Ways to Protect Your Future* by Don Silver, List Price: $14.95

- *Becoming a Category of One: How Extraordinary Companies Transcend Commodity and Defy Comparison* by Joe Calloway, List Price: $24.95

- *Beyond Success: Building a Personal, Financial and Philanthropic Legacy* by Randall J. Ottinger, List Price $27.95

- *Culture.com: Building Corporate Culture in the Connected Workplace* by Peg Neuhauser, Ray Bender & Kirk Stromberg, List Price: $27.95

- *Good to Great: Why Some Companies Make the Leap and Others Don't* by Jim Collins, List Price $27.50

- *Independent Business Ownership: Navigating to Your New Destination* by Sydney LeBlanc and Lyn Fisher, List Price: $34.95

- *Minding Our Own Business: Solving Problems Unique to Family Businesses* by Evan Hanson, Victor Nelson, List Price $14.95

- Opportunity: Your Blueprint for Financial Success by Jeff Fehrman, CFP®, List Price: $19.95

- *Seeking Succession: How to Continue the Family Business Legacy* by Loyd H. Rawls, List Price $39.95

- *Take Your Business to the Next Level: A 90 Day Plan for Achieving a Breakthrough* by Duncan MacPherson & David Miller, List Price $34.95

- *The $50,000 Business Makeover Marathon featuring the Masterminds of Marketing* (8 Audio Cassettes), List price, $99.00

- *The A-Z Alliance Marketing Kit: The Million Dollar Strategy that Costs Only Pennies* created by Dr. Lynda Falkenstein, List Price $199.00

- *The Power of Appreciation in Business* by Noelle C. Nelson, Phd, List Price $24.95

- *The Succession Bridge: Key Manager Succession Alternatives for Family Owned Businessess* by Lloyd H. Rawls, ChFC, CLU, MSFS, List Price $39.95

- *THINK BIG, Act Small: How America's Best Performing Companies Keep the Start-Up Spirit Alive* by Jason Jennings, List Price $24.95

- *Winning Clients in a Wired World: 7 Strategies For Growing Your Business Using Technology and the Web* by Kip Gregory, List Price $49.95